Praise for *Voices for Diversity and Social Justice*

"This book fills a very important void in the field of education. The editors have done a masterful job connecting poems, essays, memoirs, short stories, and visual art to promote diversity and social justice in education. I highly recommend this book for all who care about the power of education to change the world." —**Chance W. Lewis**, PhD, Carol Grotnes Belk Distinguished Professor of Urban Education; director, the Urban Education Collaborative, University of North Carolina at Charlotte

"This anthology honors the multitude of stories that are alive in our culture, and that need to be heard. Writers both well-known and unknown tell their truths in poetry and prose. They make beauty; they call out for understanding or change. I am reminded of my many years working as a poet in the schools, of the beauty and joy and learning that happen when everyone is encouraged to make art, when everyone's truth is respected, and listened to. I believe this book will do good work in the world, and will awaken its readers to values we should and could hold dear in schools everywhere." —**Deborah Keenan**, poet and professor, Creative Writing Programs, Hamline University

"TEchoing from classrooms, schools, and communities across this country come voices of rationality and justice. The words on these pages by the authors speak volumes to everyone. I was moved to read this text, and am so moved that I view many of these poems as required reading and reflection points for all who are concerned with social justice." — **Robert W. Simmons III**, professor, Loyola University Maryland

"Anyone in or around the education field needs to read Voices for Diversity and Social Justice. This anthology captures the modern moments of students in grades K-12, and college, who do not identify with their school's norms of identity, experience, or behavior. In poignant prose and powerful poetry, a tale of educational events from the 1950's through today is woven seamlessly, told through multiple voices and various perspectives. And yet, the narrative is cohesive, suggesting that while many things have changed in the last 65 years, some things remain. The feeling that the young trailblazers felt as they entered white schools after the Brown vs Board decision resonates with today's students as expressed by the anonymous writer of "I Get It," who says, "You unlocked the door and let me in. I better behave." This is an anthology of voices that want to act up, of voices no longer silenced, no longer whispering, no longer raised in a meeting and then forgotten like echoes across limited time. This anthology is of voices that will continue to reverberate, in print so as not to be denied." —**Rodney Glasgow**, chief Diversity Officer, St. Andrew's Episcopal School of Potomac, MD; Founder and Chair, National Diversity Directors Institute; Chair, National Association of Independent Schools' Student Diversity Leadership Conference

Voices for Diversity and Social Justice

Voices for Diversity and Social Justice

A Literary Education Anthology

Edited by Julie Landsman,
Rosanna M. Salcedo,
and Paul C. Gorski

ROWMAN & LITTLEFIELD
Lanham • Boulder • New York • London

Published by Rowman & Littlefield
A wholly owned subsidiary of The Rowman & Littlefield Publishing Group, Inc.
4501 Forbes Boulevard, Suite 200, Lanham, Maryland 20706
www.rowman.com

Unit A, Whitacre Mews, 26-34 Stannary Street, London SE11 4AB

British Library Cataloguing in Publication Information Available

Library of Congress Cataloging-in-Publication Data

Voices for diversity and social justice : a literary education anthology / edited by Julie Landsman,
Rosanna M. Salcedo, and Paul C. Gorski.
pages cm.
ISBN 978-1-4758-0712-7 (cloth : alk. paper) — ISBN 978-1-4758-0713-4 (pbk. : alk. paper) —
ISBN 978-1-4758-0714-1 (electronic) 1. Discrimination in education—United States. 2. Minority
students—United States—Social conditions. 3. Discrimination in education—United States—Liter-
ary collections. 4. Minority students—United States—Literary collections. I. Landsman, Julie. II.
Salcedo, Rosanna M., 1972– III. Gorski, Paul.
LC212.2.V65 2015
379.2'6—dc23

2015013039

♾ ™ The paper used in this publication meets the minimum requirements of American
National Standard for Information Sciences Permanence of Paper for Printed Library
Materials, ANSI/NISO Z39.48-1992.

Printed in the United States of America

For the students, teachers, parents whose voices are rarely heard
and who know the most
Julie Landsman

To my students, past and present, from whom I've learned so much
Rosanna M. Salcedo

For the community activists whose everyday actions
are the poetry of social change
Paul C. Gorski

Contents

Foreword   xiii

Introduction   xvii

Part I: Speaking Through the Silence

1   Diz on the Way to School   3
    By Fred Arcoleo

2   I Get It   5
    By Anon

3   Between Worlds   7
    By Heidi Andrea Restrepo Rhodes

4   How I Came to Poetry   9
    By Jeanne Bryner

5   This School   11
    By Jan Buley

6   English as a Second Language at Our Lady of Guadeloupe
    Church   13
    By Jeff Lacey

Section Questions: Speaking Through the Silence   15

Part II: Experiencing Poverty

7   Telling It Like It Is   19
    *By Adaline Carlette Love, age thirteen, as told to her
    grandmother, Leslie Ball*

8   Family Matters: A Mother and Daughter's Literacy Journey   21
    By Amy D. Clark

9   The Worst Thing About Being Poor   27
    By Amy E. Harter

10 The Poster Board   29
    By Carol L. Revelle

11 Dress to Impress   31
    By Salvador "Chato" Hernandez

12 [Untitled]   33
    By Tricia Gallagher-Geurtsen

Section Questions: Experiencing Poverty   35

Part III: Unleashing Youth's Voices

13   What If Cornel West Was Wrong?   39
     By Becky Martinez

14   Ramón's Truth   41
     By Fred Arcoleo

15   Girl on Fire   45
     By Cathleen Cohen

16   Appalachian by Proxy   47
     By Althea Webb

17   Language, The Truest Tongue   51
     By Barbara Tramonte

18   talking blocks   53
     By Cindy L. Prater

19   Skin   55
     By Tessa Stark

Section Questions: Unleashing Student Voices   57

Part IV: Being the Target

20   Survival   61
     By Lorena German

21   Star Student   63
     By Emily Brooks

22   Equations   69
     By Cathleen Cohen

23   looking in the mirror in elementary school   71
     By Sidrah Maysoon

24   The Tower, the Book, and the Girl They Let In: A Fable on
     Blackness and Racial Equity in the Academy   73
     By Shannon Gibney

25   To Lumpia or to Not Lumpia?: A Counterstory of a
     Multicultural Racial Microaggression   83
     By Cheryl E. Matias

26   The New Girl   87
     By Sheila O'Connor

Section Questions: Being the Target   89

Part V: Claiming Our Space and Identities

27 White Hallways   93
    By Cora-Lee Conway

28 First Generation College Blues   95
    By Rosanna M. Salcedo

29 Learning Up Front   101
    By Curtis Robbins

30 The Way I Am   103
    By Min Feldman

31 Independence Day   105
    By Elizabeth L. Sammons

32 America   109
    By Lauren Gatti

33 A Cultural Frankenstein   115
    By Pao "Aegean" Yang

34 Spirit First, Consequences Second: The Politics of Gender
    and Culture in the Playground   117
    By Xamuel Bañales

35 Forced Out at School: The Tenth Grade   123
    By Erica Lenti

36 Torn   125
    By Jia Curry-Bild

Section Questions: Claiming Our Space and Identities   129

Part VI: Celebrating the Power of Teachers

37 Testimony   133
    By Tasha Gaff

38 Seat Them with Princes   135
    By Jeanne Bryner

39 Finding the Strength in the Fragile   139
    By Kristy Pierce

40 Piling On: One Teacher's Journey Toward Social Justice   145
    By Lisa Cech

Section Questions: Celebrating the Power of Teachers   155

**Part VII: Reaching Across Difference and Celebrating
        Diversity's Richness**

41 People-Colored Crayons   159
    By Julie Feng

42 "Red Light, Green Light"   161
   By DJ Savarese

43 Walking Down the Corridor Is Being in Another Country   163
   By Julie Landsman

44 A Visit to the County Special Ed Program   165
   By Mary Langer Thompson

45 Breaking the Ice   167
   By Lisa Richter

46 Chasing Butterflies and Catching Grasshoppers   169
   By Elizabeth E. Vaughn

47 Breaking Bread   181
   By Merna Ann Hecht

Section Questions: Reaching Across Difference and Celebrating
   Diversity's Richness   185

Part VIII: Subversive Teaching and Learning

48 How I Learned to Read the Word   189
   By Francisco Rios

49 Even Kings   193
   By Richard Holinger

Section Questions: Subversive Teaching and Learning   201

Foreword

Beyond the clamor of the noisy school reformers—the marketers and the bankers with their hedge-fund homies—beneath the clutter of educational policy, and below the radar of the paid chattering pundits and the boisterous, bottom-feeding politicians, lies something elegant and precious: a teacher and a student in a relationship; an endless journey in a going world, filled with discovery and surprise; an ethical and intellectual transaction underway. It's the universe of teaching and learning, the domain of schools and classrooms, and it's brought to life, quietly and simply, in millions and millions of daily encounters in every corner of the globe. This is the country of the young—dazzling, trembling, and real— and it's also the province of *Voices for Diversity*.

Teaching is always practiced in a specific site, a tangible here and now, always brought to life in the mud and muck of the dynamic, surging, transient, imperfect, and fugitive spaces we share—this community or another, this prairie or that field, this classroom or that other one, this street or that pathway. But whatever intersections we occupy, wherever we find ourselves tossed up on the shores of history, if we are to be conscientious, fair, and effective we must open our eyes to those who are all around us.

Voices for Diversity awakens us by assuming that every child or youth comes to school with a heart and a mind and a body, a wide range of experiences, hopes, and dreams, a big interior life and a depth of agency that must somehow be taken into account. The editors stake out a powerful moral position here: every student—every human being—is of infinite and incalculable value, each a unique intellectual, emotional, physical, spiritual, and creative force. It's wrong—inaccurate and dishonest as well as unjust and corrupt—to assume that human beings can be known by their statistical profiles (age, race, income, test score) or understood without listening systematically to how they explain themselves, how they see the world, and what they make of what they have heard and seen. And so they listen, they observe, they invite participation.

Voices for Diversity acknowledges that there's wisdom in the room, and it illuminates—for teachers, parents, students, community members— what's possible when that wisdom is recognized and unleashed. It reminds us that a teaching identity is built in the cauldron of a classroom, and it focuses from the very start on youngsters: How do they learn? What are their preferences? If they could choose, what would they do?

How do they see things? What strengths and interests do they bring with them into the classroom? What do they think about the large goals and stated purposes of their school? More than any textbook or theory, more than adherence to a specific philosophy or ideology, we invent and reinvent ourselves as teachers through these kinds of questions, and our students are our essential guides and cocreators; they become teachers of their teachers.

We begin to improvise. We might not like ourselves—or even recognize ourselves—as tightly wound task-masters and petty dictators, and so we loosen up and slow down; we learn how to be with students in a more authentic way, more alive in our own enthusiasms and preferences and responses.

All students come to school with questions: *Who am I in the world? How did I get here? What are my chances and my choices?* The arts allow youth to assemble tentative answers to these and other questions, and over time to develop more sophisticated and dynamic ones. The arts offer an invitation to become the agent of your own story, the author of your own life, or the actor in your own film as opposed to some anonymous walk-on in someone else's worn out and clichéd script.

Author, actor, agent, composer—these roles allow youth to wield essential tools against propaganda, political agendas, dogma, and all manner of impositions and stereotypes. Art seeks honesty and authenticity, and that means it dives into contradiction, disagreements, silences, negation, denials, inconsistencies, confusion, challenges, turmoil, puzzlement, commotion, ambiguities, paradoxes, disputes, uncertainty, and every kind of muddle. That makes art an ally of critical and engaged and vibrant minds—free minds for free people. Art enhances a sense of being fully human, a work-in-progress born into an infinite and expanding star-map.

For Emily Dickinson, "Imagination lights the slow fuse of possibility," and for the great Chicago poet Gwendolyn Brooks, "Art hurts. Art urges voyages." The voyages art demands lie at the very heart of our humanness: journeys in search of new solutions to old problems, explorations of spirit spaces and emotional landscapes, trips into the hidden meanings and elaborate schemes we construct to make our lives understandable and endurable, flights hooked on metaphor and analogy, wobbly rambles away from the cold reality of the world we inhabit—the world as such—into worlds that could be or should be standing just beyond the next horizon. These are the voyages that foreground the capacities and features that mark us as creatures of the imaginary, uniquely *human* beings. Invention, aspiration, self-consciousness, projection, desire, ingenuity, moral reflection and ethical action, courage and compassion, and commitment—all of these and more are harvests of our imaginations. And our imaginations are encouraged, nourished, and fired with art.

These are journeys, then, not of acolytes but of pilgrims and explorers—we are travelers across continents and into the worlds of outer space, into the deepest recesses of our own consciousnesses and to the outer limits of our own imaginations. Explorers in the worlds of art and politics, ethics and history and more, we must also always attend to the details of ordinary existence—cooking and shopping and taking care of the children and the elders.

What are we? Where do we come from? How did we get here? Where do we want to go? This is the territory of the mind's eye and the heart's desire. This is where we enliven our values and enact our ethical judgments.

All children deserve opportunities to interrogate the universe and to develop a sense of the unique capacity of human beings to shape and create reality in concert with conscious purposes and plans. This means that our schools need to be transformed to provide children ongoing opportunities to exercise their resourcefulness, to solve the real problems of their communities, to speak up and act out. Like all human beings, children and young people need to be of use—they cannot productively be treated as "objects" to be taught "subjects." Their cognitive juices will begin to flow if and when their hearts, heads, and hands are engaged in improving their daily lives and their surroundings, speaking their own unique truths and constructing their own realities.

This is the ethical core as well the political stance of *Voices for Diversity*: no power is too big to challenge, no injustice too small to ignore. It is markedly on the side of the child, and on the side as well of the kind of dissent, rebellion, and upheaval that works to replace greed, repression, hierarchy, surveillance and control with community, peace, simple fairness, and love—all kinds of love for all kinds of people in every situation. The radical message of *Voices for Diversity* is simply this: pay attention, be astonished, choose love.

Bill Ayers

Introduction

So often the voices of the children are missing from conversations about education. So often the voices of teachers are absent from "expert" advice about how to close gaps or whether to turn around schools. So often the poetry of protest, the short story of epiphany, the memoir of families and the complex relationships that they entail are missing from the literature about education and social justice. We rarely hear the laments, the anger, the protests, or the reflections of those who are on the front lines, who teach in the classrooms or reside in these rooms as students unless we actively look for them. Otherwise they are drowned out by political blathering, by lofty pronouncements often by people whose feet haven't crossed a school threshold in decades. And as education becomes more and more regimented, with prescribed lesson plans and teacher scripts, as high-stakes tests rather than student-centered instruction remain the focus of school, the voices of children, youth, parents, and teachers are increasingly silenced. So we actively looked for them. This book is our attempt to challenge that silencing, to carve out some space, to upend all that is happening to take the humanity out of education.

When we discussed what we wanted in this anthology, we were sure we must include poetry, fiction, memoir, essay, and visual art. Precisely because the space for creative expression in schools is withering away, we wanted to create space for that expression. Years ago, we remember, schools often invited poets and other artists into classrooms; often these artists shared an entire week or more with young people. Today such residencies are rare, and they are rarest in schools with high percentages of students of color and low-income students. After-school creative writing groups that worked with neighborhood poets—once abundant in many parts of the country—have been phased out to allow more after school hours on subjects that are tested under federal education policy.

In order to stake our claim with artists and the arts, in order to advocate and celebrate activist-artist expression, we have compiled this anthology to include contributions from people who feel passionately about their own lives in schools, on the streets on the way to schools, in school parking lots, through front doors, and in the auditoriums of our educational institutions. We invited poets and short-story writers, memoirists, and painters and photographers to have their say. We bring together those who have been silenced—as teacher and artist, as child and poet.

Those who have experienced school as people in poverty, from Appalachia to Los Angeles, from Minneapolis to the suburbs of Atlanta, have their say here. Those who are blind and who experience homelessness, who are gay or bisexual or transgender are here too, sharing their stories. African American young men ask to be considered fully human here, while white southern lawyers reflect on their long lives of segregation and what has become of this fight.

When we put out a call nationally for submissions we had no idea we would receive more than four hundred works of visual art, text, and photographs. We had so many works of quality we asked to make our collection of work into two books instead of the one originally contracted. This book, *Voices for Diversity and Social Justice*, reflects the thoughts and words of those who wrote about race, culture, sexual orientation, gender, and poverty and how marginalized they could become around any of these categories. The other book, *Talking Back, Looking Forward*, reflects the thoughts and works of those looking at a broader context of educational policy. Both books use creative writing as their mode of expression. Our writers come from elementary classrooms, be they students or teachers, to high schools and even college environments. They have in common a concern for social justice, for the work of the day to day. They have in common a passion for the dignity of children, for educational equity, for the fight it takes to bring about the liberation of all of our citizens. They write of alienation, rebellion, absences, and moments of joyous inclusion. They have a deep and abiding interest in historical truth. Each, in his or her own way, unflinchingly tell the stories and songs of their lives in our schools.

Often, marginalized students have told us that when they come into the school building they leave "their real selves" at the door and are expected to assume the persona of the good student, the quiet, compliant student. When the day is over and they leave for the evening, they become "their real selves again," hear the speech of their friends and family in the foreground, feel connection to those who understand them, no matter how difficult life may be at the time. When we see what schools often use as curriculum, activities, ritual or pedagogy, we do not see represented the "real world" of a majority of our students. Thus the rupture. We do not see their interests, their music, their cadences or song, their passions, their concerns anywhere in the books or pictures or dynamic of the classroom. There are some excellent schools that are reaching out into the neighborhoods, towns, streets around them to construct themes and material, books and activities that are made central to the work of their students. These are courageous places, shifting the paradigm and centering students and their communities in their very structure. This book provides not only examples of what happens when such connections are not made, but also includes what comes about when a teacher truly connects with a student, when a parent feels heard, when a child is made to feel beautiful.

This is not a textbook, or a how-to, or a formulaic guide to creating high testing schools. Rather it is an example of the brilliance of those who are already in our classrooms and how they do their job each winter morning, each June afternoon. They may be students eager to present their poster projects. They may be teachers providing a place for students to talk about their brother who was wounded, a parent who is threatened with deportation, a gay student who is determined to claim his place in his elite high school. There are photos that capture our buildings, paintings that show our complex interaction with our institutions.

This is a book that brings the reader into the heartbeat of the buildings, the playgrounds, the offices in schools. Here are voices of social action.

Perhaps, then, it *is* a textbook, a book of text that captures reality, without jargon, without privileging the white or powerful but rather makes a space for all voices from all neighborhoods. Perhaps then, it is the ideal text for those teachers, those policy makers, those young people who honor poetry, color, story. Our idea was to provide a space for such expression, and we thank all those who sent us their words and made this idea a reality. Our belief is that this book might reach those in our institutions more readily than all the traditional scholarship texts available. It is also our hope that you, our reader, will find the piece here that moves you, the picture that makes you nod your head in recognition. And then, that moves you to listen to those who are activists in the schools and towns and cities, and encourages you to create change in the deepest parts of our system of education. There are books, magazines, Zines, performances, films, in all our schools right now. Perhaps we can make them front and center to our work together. Perhaps this book is just one beginning.

Part I

Speaking Through the Silence

In a room where
people unanimously maintain
a conspiracy of silence,
one word of truth
sounds like a pistol shot.

—Czesław Miłosz

But I suppose the most revolutionary act one can engage in is . . . to tell
the truth.
—Howard Zinn, *Marx in Soho: A Play on History*

No matter that patriotism is too often the refuge of scoundrels. Dissent,
rebellion, and all-around hell-raising remain the true duty of patriots.
—Barbara Ehrenreich

ONE

Diz on the Way to School

By Fred Arcoleo

You shake yourself awake from your cockroach dream
and find you're fetid   but human
(you even sniff as if to say *only humans can recognize their rot*)

You pull on yesterday's jeans   billowing over your sugar cane legs
and lace up your one dope pair of sneakers
nice and loose   rubbing the sides for luck
trying in vain to keep 'em looking new
'cause Pop is cheap when he doesn't have a job
Put on your best and only (puffy) coat   zip it up over your mouth
and take to the streets   it's cold outside

Something about touching down on the sidewalk that says
yeah I'm alive   fuck 'em whatever   so you walk

Walk past Ricky's house where the dogs always bark at you
In your dream their saliva drips down on you like lava
blurring a thousand eyes

    shake yourself awake again
    HUMAN   HUMAN

Roll past the Phone Express where Pop calls Mami and says *soon baby soon*
like a visit to a jail cell   all the while he's peering back at you with those don't-
you-dare eyes

    ALIVE   the sidewalk

You're 2pac throwing down a rhyme swinging your arms   *you cold as ice it's nice*
Cold now swinging your god damn arms see?
human HUMAN can't catch me

Blow right in to Billy's bodega where the fan's always blowing
And they smile at you because they know you live around here
and they know your Pop and two older brothers
you say *yo one o' those* and point   they say *ok*
and you leave with some Starburst or a pack of gum (it's the gesture
and the fact of having something that gives you confidence)

Now you slow and look around   hear your hair brushing against the nylon of your
    coat
like someone wants to drill into-the-back-of-your-head-for-a-second–*QUICK!*

    NO   Diz for Díaz not for dizzy

You're usually the first to the corner   your friends stay in the dream—sometimes
    all day but you
hurt when you don't blink your eyes and when they're red and dry
HUMAN you glare as you sniff the air   watch the white cloud—air not smoke

Yeah you see them   you wait for them   nod grin   mumble
flatten coats against each other *sssssss* as you say *I'm out*
and their voices push you away jealously *AHHHHHH*

But now you're still   staring up at the flat brick and columns and cement
and a tower   the school has a guard tower!
and windows—so many little windows   like each kid's got their own room   but
they don't

You're feeling for your hands in your pockets   making halfhearted fists
thinking of Mami down there   her little voice rubbing your ear for luck
Nene do good in school plees   you want to tell her *you can't do good in this school*

You take one last long sniff of clean air and moan
jam your hands all the way in   duck your head down
and plow into the building   feeling the last human step off the sidewalk
making it echo as you enter   *HUMAN HUMAN*
as the silence inside tries to shrink you down

TWO
I Get It

By Anon

I've been wrong
All this time
Thinking I had a right
to think;
Believing I had voice and validity
Thanks for the education, the opportunities, the financial aid
The awe of it.
I guess I am here because you decided to let me.
You had an epiphany, maybe, a lucid moment about the balance of things,
the curve of the universe.
You unlocked the door and let me in.
I better behave.
I won't bite the hand that feeds.
Do you have any idea how it would impact our budget . . .
I won't defend those of us who suffer daily little deaths because of careless
natures.
But I didn't mean it like that . . .
I won't speak out when I am exposed, embarrassed, offended.
HOW
DARE
YOU?
I've been allowed.
In the absence of power there is only the grace of God.
And, in this place, God is not me.

THREE

Between Worlds

By Heidi Andrea Restrepo Rhodes

In 1981, my father believed
in the singularity of our child tongues

and so my mother's language was
exiled from our mouths,
and the 500 years old memories with it.

In 1993, I had begun to bleed
and was horrified at the rivers I shed,
centuries of water cemeteries
telling their stories from inside me
like a scarlet tanager choking on secrets

and I was lost. Between worlds,
I had no words for these unmarked routes,
and the homogenizing literatures
whose pages we tore in restless exercise
gave no respite, while the only history
they needed us to know did not
comprehend how to pronounce our names,
or even deem them worth stumbling over.

Tagged by our skin, and
the peregrinations of our vocabularies, we were
showered with execration, the confetti fall
of graffiti and paper, telling us to go back,
go back where we came from, and still,

monolingualism fettered me,
as an orphan to the silence of his origins.

That was when the white girls wanted me dead
for being smarter than some of them, and
they decorated my hair with oranges and egg yolk, and
in the wilderness of the girls' bathroom,
in between classes, the Brown girls cornered me
in a choke-hold, cursing me for thinking I was
too deluxe to let Quetzalcoatl dream in my mouth.

Little did they know what had been stolen from me,
my tongue fighting archaic expulsions:

how much I yearned
for history to return to its home
in the spaces between my teeth,
where snake-birds and jaguars dreamed
the providence of our tomorrows
in infinite tongues,
hissing, growling, screeching
the articulations of all our names,
which have always been
worthy

of being learned.

FOUR

How I Came to Poetry

By Jeanne Bryner

My seventh grade English teacher stands with her back
to the blackboard taps her pointer against her palm.
It's no accident our hands are folded, prayerful.
She hates the Beatles, and one day even pulled her thin hair
down to her nose played a pretend guitar
screaming Yeah, Yeah, Yeah
wanting us to learn proper placement of commas.
I'm in the row under the clock, where once she saw me
peek at its face. *Time passes,* she said, *will you?*
Today she's pulled another question from her iron kettle.
When you grow up, what do you want to be?
And when Henry Johns says fireman someone laughs
in the second row. (A Negro fireman?) The undertaker's
kid says lawyer (he's such a brown noser) and of course
Lucy softly says a mom. Finally, she calls on me, a doctor
or a nurse I say. Her knuckles blanch she sighs.
To be a doctor, you have to be really smart.
Henry Johns throws me a gap-toothed grin,
a ladder to get us safely out
me and this little wren I been carrying in my chest.

FIVE

This School

By Jan Buley

We line up obediently
itchy pleated skirts with hand me down hems
Tugging nervously at soiled cuffs
    on our issued white shirts

Our chestnut eyes search the sterile hallway for clues:
whispers of sweetgrass,
bits of sinew
cedar clippings
odours long erased by ammonia bleach.
Our names eradicated in this echoing hallway.

The tall one with the clicking heels turns to us:
You'll speak only English here.
And if you loose your Ojibway tongue in my presence —
Then snip snip
Two braids fall from her vulturous fingers.

SIX

English as a Second Language at Our Lady of Guadeloupe Church

By Jeff Lacey

In a bare-walled classroom
above the new gym
twenty-eight students waited for me
to explain the past tense
of the verb *to be*.

they were

come in from
the cold air of warehouses
where all day
the glossy bodies of cows
floated wordlessly by on hooks;

he was

a hand with blood caked into
the creases of his fingernails
moving a pencil across a blank page
(small cuts into a white flank)
and when he looked at you
you were sized up, never enough;

she was

the soft rocking of her baby
in the carrier at her feet

and when we were too far past translation
her baby stirred
but she never quit listening;

it was

a new word floating out over them
and the sound of voices trying and retrying,
a trudging through January,
a working;

we were

frost on the stained glass behind us—
a fresh design, wanting to belong;

I was

in a bare walled classroom
above the new gym
trying to explain the past tense
of the verb *to be.*

But I was too young, and failed them.

Section Questions: Speaking Through the Silence

1. How are the writers of the poems that make up this section made to feel outsiders when they enter school? Have you ever felt such alienation anywhere in your life?
2. Rhodes, Buley, and Lacey write about having to suppress the language of their home, their family. What can schools do to make sure students can learn English and succeed in the world, yet also hold their home languages close, respected?
3. In Arcoleo's poem, "Diz on the Way to School," he capitalizes the word HUMAN throughout. Why do you think he does this? How does the poem work to center around his struggle to be considered human?

Part II

Experiencing Poverty

If you're in trouble, or hurt or need—go to the poor people. They're the only ones that'll help—the only ones.
—John Steinbeck, *The Grapes of Wrath*

Poverty is the worst form of violence.
—Mahatma Gandhi

The test of our progress is not whether we add more to the abundance of those who have much; it is whether we provide enough for those who have too little.
—Franklin D. Roosevelt

SEVEN

Telling It Like It Is

By Adaline Carlette Love, age thirteen, as told to her grandmother, Leslie Ball

Being homeless is having mom pick us up from school in the middle of the day with no warning and finding everything at home mostly packed and we are moving to another state.

Being homeless is not getting to say goodbye to any of my friends.

Being homeless is sleeping in a van when it is super cold and there are holes in the van because Dad crashed it. It is really crowded with three kids and Mom and Dad and Dad's friend Joe.

Being homeless means riding the bus late on a school night because we are staying at Dad's friend D's and we have to go there late so the manager won't see us.

Being homeless means attending twelve schools by sixth grade.

Being homeless is being in a shelter and Mom not sticking to her word to stay away from Dad even though she was told and warned not to see our dad again. I felt we could have gone on and had a better chance but she felt she had to go back. Since she did go back we were homeless again.

There were times I sort of wanted to hide it. I was disappointed we were homeless and I felt it was my fault because I was the first one born and my mom could have had a better life and waited and had me later. I *know* it is not my fault, but I *feel* like it is.

19

Being homeless is moving around a lot and making new friends to start with and getting all excited and finally getting the hang of things and figuring out how everything works and then it's gone.

Changing schools so much just made me feel really dumb. It made me way behind and I didn't want to participate. It made me a shy person and I'm not like that at all.

Since we were homeless we had to stay at other people's houses and they would kick us out and there was a lot of fighting about it.

When people decided to kick us out we would have nowhere to go and we would just walk around all night. We would go to the playground because there was a light there.

When we were homeless there was a lot more drama that would start as an argument and go into big time fighting.

One time there was Joseph and Joseph's girlfriend Cici. Mom and Cici got really drunk and tried to leave and take us kids with them. Everyone got into a big huge fight. The worst part was seeing the women get hurt.

The last place we were staying was on the reservation with my auntie. All the houses out there are pretty much dirty and there is lots of trash in the yards but one day we went walking on a really long walk and we started to see these nicer houses that got nicer and nicer and no trash in the yards and my auntie said it was white people and she got really mad and she kept saying why did these white people say this is our land and now they come and live here. Lots of people were staring but she just kept saying why did the white people come here and I was just like there you are a Native preacher telling it like it is.

EIGHT

Family Matters

A Mother and Daughter's Literacy Journey

By Amy D. Clark

I was born to a sixteen-year-old mother from a broken home in the coal-fields of central Appalachia, where unemployment, poverty, and illiteracy rates are reportedly among the highest in the nation. If my mother and I were the statistics we are supposed to be, we would look something like this:

She would be a high-school dropout and single mother with two or more children by age twenty. She would be in an abusive relationship that she would not leave because she had no support. Her prospects for employment would be grim because there are few jobs. For such a woman, with no money, no support system, and a low level of functional literacy, college would be an unlikely dream.

Simply because I am her daughter, and no one in my family had ever attended college, I would continue this cycle with my own children. For us, "Appalachia" would be a place to escape, and "culture" would be an abstract word with no meaning. "School" would be a place where we don't belong because there is no place in a standardized test for voices like ours.

I have heard that numbers don't lie, but neither are they entirely truthful. Yes, there are too many girls and women who fall into these categories in our region, but my mother and I do not. The reality is that she completed her GED and slowly worked her way through college while raising two children.

Her love of reading led her to a degree in library science, then two Master's degrees, and finally a doctoral program. She and my father are still happily married after forty years, and she coaches elementary teachers on how to teach reading in a community on the Virginia–Kentucky border. They raised a daughter who is an associate professor at a liberal arts college, and a son who is a successful businessman.

Our literacy lives have grown and intertwined over the years like tendrils on a vine; I inherited her love of books and reading, which also inspired my love of writing. This past summer, after years of nudging, she joined the Appalachian Writing Project's newest cohort as a teacher-consultant. As founding director of the Appalachian Writing Project, I am proud to call her a colleague.

Home-to-School Literacy Connection

When I began to examine the powerful connection between the literacies of home and school, I realized why she and I defied the odds.

Because I was born to such a young mother, and because I grew up in a collectivist society where family ranks second only to God, my love of words was nurtured by *three* generations, my first literacy coaches—none of whom had a college degree—who taught me how to see the world by reading and writing my way to understanding.

We can't deny the power of statistics in determining who gets to attend college, how resources are allocated, how mainstream America perceives rural students, and, most importantly, how rural students *see themselves*.

But I don't trust quantitative descriptions of people, particularly those from rural areas, and more specifically those in the poorest parts of Appalachia. Numbers ignore the most important aspects of rural culture, such as dialect and the plurality of literacies that children learn at home, because these things cannot be measured.

So let this be *our* truth:

Many of us leave and return to Appalachia to live because our roots grow deep, and because growing up in these mountains means no matter where we go in the world, we are anchored spiritually to that place of voice and story and song.

The writing project showed me that I needed to come back to the area and teach because I know my students' culture. I know the tension between being Appalachian and becoming "standardized" by tests, prejudice, and the pressure to escape the pitfalls and challenges that exist there.

Despite an assessment movement that seeks to categorize and analyze, I want to convince teachers to take into account the deep, abiding influence of place on rural students. Kentucky author George Ella Lyon calls this juncture of region and writing the "voiceplace." Most importantly, teachers need to know that they stand in the middle of a long line of people who began their students' educations long before these students reached the classroom.

My education began in the most unlikely of places: a single-wide trailer at my grandmother's farm on the Virginia/Kentucky border, which sat along one mile of Long Hollow. It was here that my parents, my grandmother, and my great-grandmother laid the foundation for my love of culture and teaching, and my future research.

My days at home were filled with books and drawing (my mother is a talented painter) and song (my dad is a talented singer). On Fridays, I read *Reader's Digest* condensed books at my grandmother's house, then walked a path through the woods to my great-grandmother's farm, where sets of Nancy Drew, Trixie Belden, and Archie comics awaited. As if that weren't enough, my great-grandmother fed me hearty helpings of folk tales and preaching, along with her country cooking.

Research supports this home-to-school literacy connection.

Some kids may despise grammar and diagramming worksheets, as I did, but they know syntax, phonology, and vocabulary well enough to code-switch or use a formal voice when they want to avoid prejudice.

Likewise, nonmainstream dialect speakers (such as those speaking Appalachian English) have already learned to use the complicated linguistic patterns of their home voice as well as a more standard variety. Teachers may assume, then, that their students are bringing "well-developed linguistic abilities" to the classroom.

Author Lee Smith writes that the King James Bible is the most influential book for a southern writer. Kids in chiefly Protestant central Appalachia may not adore Shakespeare (I didn't) but they can recite fluently the King James Bible, a book that was translated into Elizabethan English by the same king who was a patron of Shakespeare's acting company. Appalachian kids hear this version of English weekly in church.

Author Silas House writes that growing up in an Appalachian church and hearing the poetic sermons is one of the reasons he became a writer. Relics of Elizabethan English were—and still are—common in the sermons at the Victoria Freewill Baptist Church where I grew up, and recited in prayers over my parents' kitchen table. The phonology and lexicon of Shakespeare's era were as familiar to me as my own voice, but I needed someone to make that connection.

The Richness of Rural Life

Some kids may not be fluent in foreign languages but they can speak in multiple dialects, drawing from their tacit knowledge about language and their understanding of its politics in a place where sounding "different" can mark you as an outsider. Their home voice, that dialect we call Appalachian English, has its own system of grammar and vocabulary.

They know and use grammar, just a different kind. They need someone to make that connection.

I spent hours listening to my great-grandmother tell stories on her front porch. She spoke in an uncompromising Appalachian dialect that was pure as poetry. She used phrases I rarely hear now ("It's nigh time we was gettin' to bed") and her stories were rich with artifacts of a language peppered with patterns such as "There ain't many more of us that remember the old ways" that date back to Chaucer's era.

My grandmother, mother, and I still speak in this voice when we want to return to our comfortable tongue, like a pair of well-worn shoes. Sadly, I wouldn't learn of my linguistic history until college, where I took a class called Appalachian Prose and Poetry, but I encourage teachers to begin teaching about it in elementary school.

Rural students may not like science worksheets, but they know the anatomy and life cycle of a tobacco plant and how to grade the leaves on a cold October night in their daddy's barn. They may not enjoy dissecting in a lab but they can catch a fish or kill a deer and name every part as they carve and harvest the meat.

They know the earth is synchronized with the heavens, which affects growth and cycles. My great-grandmother's recipe book, which my grandmother and mother still use, is filled with facts and figures for recipes, home remedies, and planting and harvesting by the astrological signs. What a wonderful bridge to science, like Homer Hickam's boyhood fascination with the heavens, which gave him such rich material for writing and led to a career with NASA.

They may not like math, but they can calculate the length of a pine board needed to build a porch, follow fractions on a recipe for canning heirloom tomatoes, or use geometry to design a quilt. Phobic about math since the fourth grade when I began my struggle, I knew that it wasn't something you got at school. I watched my relatives, some whose formal education ended in an elementary grade, calculate fluently for woodworking, sewing quilts and clothes, or keeping budgets, and all with no calculator. I needed someone to show me the bridge from there to the classroom.

You may not see them in band class, but three nights a week rural kids are standing on a church stage glorifying with a guitar or piano. Music was around me my entire life. My dad and grandpas played the guitar, and my granny played the fiddle.

I understand why numbers are important. I know that's how some people think and see the world, the same way I use words to make meaning. But if numbers are all you have for creating a profile of a rural student or gauging literacy, you'll miss the point entirely.

Even as a teenager my mother knew I needed music and books and crayons and paper. She and my grandmothers read and praised my poems and stories. When my first poem was published in a national magazine she was my biggest fan. I was fifteen, the same age as she when she discovered that she would be a mother—and decided that we would *not* be statistics.

"Mom, You Are *a Writer"*

For me, writing is a pleasant experience; for my mother, it's far from cathartic. Writing unmasks insecurity caused by a painful childhood and difficult initiation into adulthood. While her childhood may have spurred her relentless ambition, it has also made personal and creative writing nearly inaccessible. It was one of the reasons she resisted the summer institute, where she would have to face down that demon once and for all.

I was nervous about our roles there, and worried about intruding into the private place that writing can be. Our roles had reversed: it was my turn to read her stories and tell her what I thought, to encourage her to trust her instincts as a writer and ignore the nagging voice that causes her to grieve over every line. She encouraged my honest—even critical— feedback. What did I think?

I remember the moment I read a piece she had written about a story from the archives of our family lore, told time and time again by my great-grandmother. It was a story about a misunderstood woodcarving woman who fled into the woods and lived in a cave after being charged with attempted murder.

I read the first line, and chills spread up my arms. I realized for the first time the pride she must have felt as a mother when she read my writing, how she must have wanted my teachers to see it, too. I'm not sure if anything I said that day sounded authentic; as her daughter, my credibility as a writing peer is probably weak at best. So, I'm saying it now: Mom, you *are* a writer.

In Appalachia, when you meet someone for the first time, she will ask you about your "people," who they are, and where they live. I learn about my students' people in writing assignments that encourage them to talk about their culture and identity. (One such assignment is Lyon's poem prompt "I Am From . . .").

To understand the literacy practices of a rural student is to understand her "people," and you won't find those answers in numbers. You will find them in lines such as, "I am from the work-worn hands of my great-grandmother, her script as delicate as lace/I am from 'arthuritis remedy' just inside the Holy Bible."

In my own life, as in that of many others in rural areas, the answers about our people and how we came to be writers span several generations to where our literacy journey began. As for my mother and me, the writing project has made us colleagues but the *writing* made us kindred spirits.

NINE

The Worst Thing About Being Poor

By Amy E. Harter

Inspired by Sherman Alexie's The Absolutely True Diary of a Part Time Indian *and Aaron Huey's Pine Ridge Reservation photography*

Unless you came up that way
You never think about how things cost more for the poor
And how every day, every second, costs inner wealth
That was long ago liquidated,
blood and money outpoured.

Naked children sit in the sink for their mothers to come lather their hair,
To come back from the daze of *just needing a moment*,
of sitting and staring
Because there are meals to make
but no money to make them,
There is only restless sleep to wake from,
With no strength left to take from,
Too much worry to shake from,
No kind lies left to fake from.

Poverty is learning that there are things that can't be spent,
Because, like Junior said, a bullet only costs two cents
Instead of the thousand to take the dog to the vet.

Life becomes the plastic garbage bag, hung on the kitchen drawer,
unintentional, but necessary, and *this is all we have space for*.
America's "Don't Stop Believin'" —plays on us all the time,
But for some of us there are no ladders left to climb,
Only mile wide gaps between the shaky tightropes we were born on
Empty air instead of opportunities to form on.

Rich kids never watch their fathers shoot a sick dog out of mercy.
A desperate insurance, saving cash in case the kids have an emergency.
Even then, there might be some money for some pills but not for surgery.
Sure makes the "You can do it!" classroom posters feel like perjury.

No shot against
Economics of choices that don't really get made,
The cry of warring hard against the loans that can't be paid.

TEN

The Poster Board

By Carol L. Revelle

In the middle age of my youth,
Differences were magnified; I ached for sameness.
Embarrassing poverty hung from my limbs—
Tattered garments surrounded by suburban plenty.
Free lunch and food stamps kept my belly full
And my humiliation raw.

And I walked around pretending.
Pretending I wasn't poor;
Pretending I didn't care.
Until confronted with an insurmountable obstacle
    One white poster board.

"Complete your project on a poster board,
And bring it to class and share," she said.
My eyes welled up, but I did not cry.
"Public education is free;
Tell that to your teacher," my parents said.
But I knew what they meant:
"Poster boards aren't sold at garage sales."

But there was a box
    a large box.
Once unpacked, I carefully cut
    a square
I completed the project with what I had
    an ink pen
But I came to my senses

and left my project at home.

Everyone shared.
Beautiful, clean, and white—
Were the bright futures of my peers.
As she checked our work,
Her lips thinned in response to my empty desk.
My eyes welled up.
I put my head down and pretended to sleep.

ELEVEN

Dress to Impress

By Salvador "Chato" Hernandez

Dress to impress is what Ms. Reed had said.

"You have to wear your Sunday best. It's a leadership conference you know. You need to make a good impression."

There he was in his finest south side attire. He smiled and walked with his head held high. He felt like one of those important men, like the ones who wear suits and work downtown.

Before he left the house that morning his mother had said "¿Y ahora tú? ¿A dónde vas que te vez tan guapo?"

Although his mother would always tell him que estaba guapo, that he was handsome, today he actually felt it.

He looked his best. He wore a black imported Italian wool suit vest. It had a six-button closure with lining and pockets. He had never heard of the brand Ludlow, but it must have been chingón, because it had been imported. Despite the fact that it was missing the top and two lower buttons, and the lining had become unsewn in the back, it was the nicest piece of clothing he had ever owned.

He liked the way his hands felt in the silky pockets, even though they both had holes in them, and anything he put in them would just fall through, and get lost in between the lining. He didn't care.

He also liked the way his pinstriped dress pants felt on his legs, smooth like hot shaving cream. To him, pinstripes made a man look more sophisticated, more important and that's why he wore them, even though they were two sizes too big. Muy chingón.

Imported Italian wool vest over a faded white t-shirt. Pinstripe dress pants that were so long, he stepped on them with his classic, black Reeboks, so faded from wear and tear, the suede had turned green. His mother had found a deal the day she bought his outfit, $10 for both the vest and dress pants at the 24th St. segunda.

As he approached Ms. Reed, he walked with a strut, as if he were walking to a podium to receive an award for "Most Chingón."

"Ms. Reed, what do you think? Chingón, huh?"

"Ricardo, I said we were going to a leadership conference. What's wrong with you?"

TWELVE

[Untitled]

By Tricia Gallagher-Geurtsen

I asked her to write about justice
She wanted to write about justice

She didn't write
She didn't write

She was too busy, trabajando mucho
Cleaning rich people's houses

Here is her story:

There.

Section Questions: Experiencing Poverty

1. In many of these poems and stories, writers talk of how they have been made to feel ashamed in school. Find the ways this happened and discuss how the teachers and schools could have handled the situations, requirements differently.
2. In Amy Harter's poem "The Worst Thing About Being Poor" she uses specific details to make it clear what poverty meant for her. What are these details? How can you describe something you feel strongly about using details to make the reader experience it too? What does the space mean?

Part III

Unleashing Youth's Voices

The extremists are afraid of books and pens. The power of education frightens them.
—#MalalaDay #EducationFirst

This is slavery, not to speak one's thought.
—Euripides, *The Phoenician Women*

Choosing with integrity means finding ways to speak up that honor your reality, the reality of others, and your willingness to meet in the center of that large field. It's hard sometimes.
—Terry Tempest Williams, *When Women Were Birds: Fifty-Four Variations on Voice*

Everything becomes a little different as soon as it is spoken out loud.
—Hermann Hesse

THIRTEEN

What If Cornel West Was Wrong?

By Becky Martinez

What if Cornel West was wrong
When he called me a serious sister
What if best intentions
Get things twisted
As a white teacher
In a classroom
Blazing radiant color
It's no wonder
Kids forced undercover
Hiding language fluencies
Sandbaggin' talents
Tagged as misfits
By misunderstanding Miss Ivories

Instead I'll be
Something different I said
But one white Ms. Martinez
Que puede hablar in Español
Mas o menos
Is more or less
A patch over what is really needed

I'm here to implore you:
The critically conscious
Poets of color
Among you
Are wise wordsmiths weaving history and literacy
With firsthand experience

You see

It ain't enough
To be named honorary sister
When DPS just lost 59 of its
Precious and diminishing
African-American teachers
Cuz even at my best
I'm not enough to supplement
The gap between 55% Latino students
And only 14% Latino teachers
For while I can expose
The cons and pros
Of power dynamics in transaction
I'll never be the image
Students need to see—
their likeness in academic,
Ass-kicking action

But I can bear witness
And confess.
In many schools
Heroes like Mali's Sundiata matter less
Than studying perpetrators of indigenous conquest—
This is what is meant
When we say discrimination's systemic

The union's still squabblin' over contract minutes
Rather than curriculum content, it's
No wonder some would 86
Teacher off their list
Of ways to fight injustice

In the meantime . . .
Would be drivers are turned to passengers
Escorted to lessons
'bout John Brown 'stead a Nat Turner
'bout Columbus 'stead a Abubakari
Kids wonderin', "Where is my history?"

and

"Where are the teachers who look like me?"

FOURTEEN

Ramón's Truth

By Fred Arcoleo

I hate Mr. Ramírez.
I hate Mr. Ramírez.
I hate Mr. Ramírez.
Him and his dumb-ass face—with pimples on it. How's a forty-year-old teacher gonna have pimples?

"I don't want you to fail," he says, sounding all sincere. Fail me! I don't care. But then he has to call my mother, like he's telling on you. Tattle-tale. I wish he was in Lavoi's class—she hated tattle-tales. She put Hector Borges in the closet that time and wouldn't let him out till the principal came. I wish I was the principal—I'd fire Ramírez.

Now I can't go anywhere for a year. How much homework can you do? It's all stupid stuff anyway. Nobody even reads it, except Ramírez. He writes so much on the paper; he writes more than you do! Half the time I don't even understand what he writes. And he uses that stupid purple marker, like he's a girl or something.

Freewriting. He always says, "Write whatever you want!" with that big-ass smile of his. What if you don't want to write anything? Ramírez thinks of everything: "Write, *'I don't want to write'* until you think of something to write." What the hell is that? If I wanted to write something I would. Don't push me. Then he got that bat book out of the library, talking about how some kids like to read about animals. I couldn't stop thinking about Yolanda and how the bats bombed her that night in D.R.[1] Mami had to swat them with her dishtowel, but Yo got all scratched up and scared. She didn't want to go out in the night or the day!

"Excellent, Ramón—write about it." Ramírez kept saying. Come on, I just *told you*: *you* write about it if you like it so much.

41

It's not like I hate writing. I like it all right, sometimes. It's just that these teachers always gotta say, "Write more." No matter how much I write—*more, more, more*. Teachers are so stupid sometimes, they can't understand a simple story. "The reader wants you to take us there," Ramírez says. What if I don't want to? I don't want everyone knowing my business. My mother finds out half the stuff I'm doing and then I really won't go out for a year. I'll get sent to D.R., like Rey did.

But some writing is kinda cool. Like that story we read in class about that kid who stole a quarter and his father chased him all around the house and when he caught him he didn't even hit him. That's pretty cool. Or the one about that kid who steals from the old lady and instead of calling the cops she brang him home and gave him food. That stuff is all right.

I hate the cops. Miguel got me mad—one time during freewriting he wrote how he got arrested outside his building and he didn't even do nothing. Everyone was feeling sorry for him, asking him when he got to go to court, and he was telling everybody in two weeks, and how he was worried about getting framed just cause he was hanging out around supposed "drug dealers." Then about a few weeks later, Ramírez said he called his mom, and it really didn't happen. That got me mad. How you gonna make up something like that, when that happens for real every day? Ramírez was mad! Said you shouldn't play around with stuff like that, even though he said it was good he wrote about it. I don't get that part. Maybe he's trying to say it's good Miguel is writing, but not about that stuff. Or, it's good he's writing, but he shouldn't pretend something like that happened to him when it really didn't. I think that's what it is. It's true. True that, Ramírez.

Wait, my mom's at the door . . .

She's gone. I told her I was writing (it's the truth, even though it's not the homework). She was glad. She said Ramírez is just trying to help. She's not nosy, really, but she's always there, at least she used to be, before she got that job. Her *career*, she calls it. Big fancy career, but what about us? Papi used to say, "Take care of the kids." She didn't listen; that's why he left. Or one reason anyway.

I remember when Papi used to come into my room when I was doing my homework and tell me a story about the old times in D.R. When he finished he would say, "Your turn," and I would tell him a story too. If I didn't know what to say, he would laugh and shout, "It's easy, make it up!" I would tell stories about dragons and monsters and mean old cats and bad little boys. Mostly they were funny, but sometimes sad too. Then he would say, "Time to finish that homework," and he would help me make the letters.

One time when we were telling stories, Papi said, "It's time we wrote down some of our truth." Truth, he called it. So we started writing the stories down, one story every night for about a week. It was hard; I couldn't hardly write then; he had to help me make the words. But he kept saying, "You can do it." Then Papi got some fancy pieces of wallpaper from his job cleaning offices and we made a book cover out of cardboard. Hey, wait . . .

I found it! It looks funny now, kind of old. The cover is peeling off. But it still has some of the gold glitter, and the title's all matted down in yarn: *Pito and Papi's Truth*. There's big globs of dried glue, like plastic! I'm gonna ask Mami for some glue to fix it up, but this time I'm only going to use a little.

The stories are funny. I can't hardly read what I wrote; the letters are all different shapes and sizes. They get big and then small, and kind of lean down toward the right. And there's weird spellings, like "speshl" for "special." And I wrote "men man" for "mean man," I think. How did Papi know what it said?

Mami comes in at night sometimes. She even helps me with my writing when I have a big project or something—or when she finds something I wrote. One time she said, "That's nice, sweetheart," but it's not the same. She's not as much fun as Papi was. And sometimes it seems like she's not really paying attention totally, like she's thinking of something else, you know?

I miss Papi.
I miss Papi.
Papi . . .
I miss you.

NOTE

1. Dominican Republic

FIFTEEN

Girl on Fire

By Cathleen Cohen

Girl on fire with siren hair,
you wrap yourself in poems,
graffiti snakes around neck and wrists,
fingers inked in cryptic words, a tangled bible.

You jangle windows, rattle doors,
shouting at the guards, who are armed.
You will not remove piercings or steely chains
or your pride will fly off in the slightest wind.

You won't meet our eyes with your eyes,
which simmer and might explode,
then stray to my arms filled with books,
offerings that might be strong enough
to quench the god of anger.

Beautiful, pierced child, enter!
We are all poets here.
Spark this room with your burning tongue.
Climb towards light on a rope of hair and sinew.
Who could not see you in all these flames?

SIXTEEN

Appalachian by Proxy

By Althea Webb

My identity is that of a Black Southern woman born in 1956. When I moved to Eastern Kentucky, I began to question that identity for the first time in my life. As a native born Kentuckian, I thought that I knew Kentucky. But, the first time I heard traditional mountain music I was awe struck by the clear, beautiful voice of Ashley Long who sang with the Berea College Bluegrass Ensemble. She was singing *You'll Never Leave Harlan Alive.* Darrell Scott's lyrics and her haunting voice brought tears to my eyes. At the time it was not clear to me why I was crying. The song tells the story of a man's great-granddaughter, she sings about the family lineage in the "deep, dark hills of eastern Kentucky" where the "sun comes up about ten in the morning and the sun goes down about three in the day" and "you spend your life just thinking how to get away." The pain and the despair was palatable in the lyrics and in the style of singing.

When I came to Berea College three years ago I thought I was accepting employment as a college professor; quickly I became aware that I had embarked on something more than a job or a "career path." I was drawn to Berea College because of the institution's 150-year history and commitment to African American students. I did not want to live in the mountains so I commuted from Lexington to Berea the first year, not telling my family that I had taken a job in the mountains of Eastern Kentucky. I knew they would worry about my living in the mountains, because of all the negative stereotypes of racist whites. After a year of commuting, I decided to move. I had found the people in town were friendly and there was a vital Black community. As I prepared to move, I joked with my Lexington friends that in a year I would be canning and quilting, after which we would all enjoy a big laugh. We knew, I was a city girl and moving to the country (as I thought at the time) was like transporting me to the moon; plus I had no intention of changing who I was, simply because I moved thirty miles away. Those thirty miles have been more like three hundred thousand.

In my first class, I had more African American students than I had taught in all thirteen years of being a college professor in Kentucky. As the semester proceeded and I got to know the white students, I found them different than other white people I had encountered. I had worked with poor whites before, but this was something beyond socioeconomic status. The white entitlement was not there, and there was a humbleness and respect I had never experienced from white students as a whole. They were outspoken about some things, and shy about other things; they were smart, but not savvy; I found contradiction after contradiction. I wanted to know my students, and I found that in talking with them about their home in rural places in Appalachia was similar to talking to an International Student about their life in developing country. I did not understand Appalachian culture. I learned that although the people were white, they were not part of the mainstream dominant white culture. Because I was working with a population group about which I knew very little, I was hungry to know more.

In my second semester I took the College's Appalachian Tour and Seminar. I thought a week-long seminar would answer all my questions about the region. Within minutes of the start of the seminar I was confused. My first question was, "Is it pronounced Appalachia (ap-uh-*laey*-chuh) or Appalachia (ap-uh-*lach*-chuh)?" I had been taught in grammar school to say -*laey*- and that -*lach*- was incorrect. Chad Berry, Appalachian Center Director, explained that those outside the region said the former, while those inside the region said the later. In that moment I decided to use the regional pronunciation. This was a place where I wanted to belong. I had already begun to feel connected and I wanted to explore those feelings in more depth. I knew I would need to reject my incorrect teachings. When I compared what I learned on the tour to what I already knew, I came to understand that my childhood education was served up with a large helping of disdain for Eastern Kentucky. I was taught what most outsiders learn, that mountain people were poor, ignorant, and backward. These negative images and stereotypes still persist today. During my childhood, whenever Kentucky made the news or was depicted in film, it was an image of an Eastern Kentuckian. I was taught that Western Kentucky suffered from a poor reputation both in our nation and internationally because Eastern Kentucky was portrayed as the whole of *Kentucky*.

Now I think of my life in terms of "before and after," before I lived on the border of Appalachia and after I spent time there. When Michael Kors, one of the judges of *Project Runway*, a reality show for aspiring designers, told Raymundo Baltazar in Season 2, Episode 3, that his design for Barbie looked like "Little Appalachian Barbie," I laughed as anyone would at a witty retort that perfectly summed up the hideous design of the outfit. Looking back on my laugher, I realize that I was like the individual who would never make a racist joke, but who would laugh when someone else made such a joke. I find this distasteful and unexpected in myself. We live in a society where you will lose your job for making a racist joke, but a society where one can make a regional slur about people and there are no consequences.

When I read Stephanie Meyers' *Twilight Saga* novels and learned that Emmett Cullen was a native of some unknown town in Appalachia in 1935, I was hesitant, and braced myself for a negative depiction of a young mountain man. As expected, Emmett is stereotypical in that he is described as big, burly, and prone to violence. If Emmett were truly Appalachian, he would have been from a specific town within that large region. Appalachia is not a homogeneous place; it matters to me if he was born in Asheville or Pikeville, if he had lived in town or in a holler. The *Twilight Saga* novels have sold in the millions, and the image of the violent hillbilly lives on for the next generation of young adults.

I began to question my own education about the region, my own biases about the people and my own complicity in not recognizing or challenging the stereotypes. I did not know that there was such beauty in the people, in land, and in the culture; I felt guilty about my ignorance. These are not poor simple people who live in the past; Appalachian culture is dynamic, vital, and very much looking to the future. I began to read as much as possible, attended cultural events in the region, and talked to everyone and anyone who would share with me their experiences of having grown up there. What I began to see was that what I knew about rural African American culture was connected to Appalachian culture in ways different from a connection to mainstream white culture. There are similarities with food, religion, family, and migration among African Americans and white Appalachians. I gained a better understanding of my students, and I began to incorporate aspects of Appalachian culture in my courses. I want to teach my students to take pride in Appalachian heritage; I want them to understand the history, the struggles, and the triumphs.

On April 15, 2010, Silas House, a writer and novelist, spoke on campus about his childhood and about how being Appalachian was an important aspect of who he was as a person. At one point he said that all of us at Berea College were Appalachian. Those who were born Appalachian and those who had moved here were now Appalachian by proxy. I was profoundly moved by this thought. I had wondered if I would ever be considered Appalachian, and I had never come to any conclusion about this. I never dared to ask. I assumed I would always be an outsider or "flatlander." While at the time I did not understand why I cried when I heard Ashley Long sing, I did understand why I became tearful when Silas House pronounced that I too was Appalachian. My home is now in Eastern Kentucky, and there are many aspects of Appalachian culture that I value and share. I came to Berea to work with African American students, but I stay because of my connection to this place, this land. I am a migrant to Eastern Kentucky, and *I will never leave Berea alive.*

SEVENTEEN
Language, The Truest Tongue

By Barbara Tramonte

A friend who teaches English in
New York City
is appalled!

One of her students writes,
"It's a doggy-dog world"
Another laments the fate of those
"who can't find they hats."

But me, I bow to their genius:
as they create their expression,
as they reveal their feelings
with a metaphor they own
   no borrowed one.

I've sat with Harvard grads and
felt like puking.
I've seen the way white people
brush the fate of Blacks off the table
like too many crumbs.

Hell, I've looked for work in New York City
down and out
and you know what Ms. B?
It's a doggy-dog world.

EIGHTEEN
talking blocks

By Cindy L. Prater

piano was the word you couldn't get me to understand
you dumped out the bucket of legos and built one
holding it up to me, *see?*
annoyance on your face

i hate the detours in our communication
the developmental glitch that takes your clear thought
launches it through static, rolling the picture like an old
antennae'd tv
until it emerges broken, garbled

as your teacher
what hurts most
is that I can't find the buttons
to adjust it
to break the code
to enable you to deliver the inputted message with the clarity
of your initial shining thought

as you labored to communicate
jamming one block onto another with intricacy and exasperation
a thought wedged unsettled

society declares me *typical*
you are zoned as *special*

if i had to build my thoughts
using my own limp fumbling spatial talents

i could not

i would hold up my piano and others would guess
box? table? doghouse?

NINETEEN
Skin

By Tessa Stark

Oh how I wish I could be brave
I wish I had the courage to say
"It doesn't matter, brown, black, or white"
Or at least it shouldn't, "because you like who you like."

Though I find that without us knowing
We judge and define, though we don't think it's showing
Instead of talking, we'll look and stare
The other thinks it's hateful, and returns a vicious glare.

We judge on race, religion, and superficial stuff
We try not to do this, but it is rather tough
We try to look not on the out, but the inside
But it's hard to look for something that you can't see with your eyes

So, in the end, we may attract each other Like magnets; love, drawing us in
But we also repulse each other Like planets; hate, based on the color of our skin

Section Questions: Unleashing Student Voices

Some of these pieces are written by teachers, some are written by students. They are all talking about trying to break the silences, to have the courage to speak. How do they express this in different ways?

1. Discuss Tricia Gallagher-Guersten's poem. It is short. It has a lot of space in it.
2. In her poem "Girl on Fire" by Cathleen Cohen, the teacher is writing to a student she wants to reach, to help express herself, to claim language. Write a letter to someone, asking that person to tell you his or her story.
3. In "Ramon's Truth" by Fred Arcoleo, Mr. Ramirez gives Ramon permission to write. He breaks through to him. How does he do this?

Part IV

Being the Target

Sometimes even to live is an act of courage.
—Seneca

Confront the dark parts of yourself, and work to banish them with illumination and forgiveness. Your willingness to wrestle with your demons will cause your angels to sing. Use the pain as fuel, as a reminder of your strength.
—August Wilson

The ultimate tragedy is not the oppression and cruelty by the bad people but the silence over that by the good people.
—Martin Luther King Jr.

TWENTY
Survival

By Lorena German

At the broken down, crusty sidewalk, pot holed intersection of Lawrence St. and Haverhill Street
I discovered the harsh realities of life.
There stood my Lawrence High.
I saw a building, I saw pride, I saw meaning falling apart.
I heard frustration laughing each time a door was slammed.
I felt depression walking around the hallways each time the bell rang.
Lined with buckets like napkins damp with teardrops falling from Heaven.
The windows tinted like Hondas that gave us a dark view of the world and made us invisible to it.
The cracks on the tile floor and wall paint echoed our cries of rage and discontentment.
Racism filled the air, a strong fragrance.
Anger came up from my heart, on the tip of my tongue, with no exit.
We were dead students walking to the auditorium.
They glared at us from high above on the stage:
"Sit down and be quiet. Look to your left and look to your right. Half of you won't be here in four years."
I stopped listening after those first words.
My blood rushed. My eyes lit up. My brain jumped. My lungs pumped.
I knew the walls made bets on who wouldn't finish this race.
The seats were there and were witnesses to how we had no place.
The mirrors gave us a cracked vision—a broken image, the only . . . Man listen!
I looked to the left and looked to the right
and asked myself,
"How will I survive?"

TWENTY-ONE

Star Student

By Emily Brooks

I stood at the front of the classroom, holding my Star Student poster and sobbing inconsolably. "Star Student" was the special project where each week, one student got to create a homemade poster and tell stories about their family, passions, and life to classmates. You'd think being the star student would become a happy proud memory among the neutral memories of early childhood. Yet for me, it exemplified everything wrong with my elementary school career.

Most of the details of the morning were the same as any other morning in second grade: I didn't take the school bus, for instance. On Star Student day, my mother drove me to school because she was so excited for me. I'd worked hard on my project, and she was proud. Getting a ride to school for other reasons was part of the routine: I missed the school bus nearly every day for two or three years straight, ever since my family had moved. You see, I was a kid with just as much fascination in the outside world as I had fears about it. Unfortunately, I had anxiety about everything from loud noises and crowds to speaking my mind and seeing the school nurse for my asthma inhaler. I didn't have my diagnosis of autism spectrum disorder then, but the traits were present: I was disconnected from my peers, and I thrived on keeping things the same. The transition of moving cross-state was daunting.

I liked my kindergarten in Pittsburgh, after all. I sat at the end of a long windy table next to my best friend from across the street, Erica. She was bold and smart and good at doing things like riding a bike without training wheels over tree roots. She protected me from harm. We walked to school together with our moms and wore our backpacks on our stomachs, laughing that we were pregnant. My original kindergarten teacher

63

Mrs. K had a smile and let me bring my baby brother (and mother) in for show-and-tell. We had shoeboxes full of our thick pencils and bright crayons and a big slide outside that a classmate fell off and had to wear a zebra eye patch. We had a hall center with wooden monkey bars, which we shared with the kindergartners next door, and we had a paper and craft center. At Halloween, we learned a song to the tune of "The Twelve Days of Christmas." Mrs. K played the piano and my goofy classmate Patrick and I rolled on laughing on the carpet: "*Two* trick-or-treaters and an *old* owl in a dead tree!" When I left, she made me a photo album with marker drawings of my classmates and snapshots of us learning and playing together.

After we moved cross-state to a place with trees and rivers and cow farms, I went into my new kindergarten classroom with expectations of similar kindheartedness and fun. Was I naive? Sure, but nobody could blame me—I was five years old.

My new kindergarten teacher, Ms. P, was unhappy to have a midyear addition to the classroom. It messed up her order and structure. I was just a kid—I was good—and I was confused. Why did this teacher stubbornly, subtly undermine me? She refused to show me where the bathroom was. I was too shy and scared to ask, so I arrived home smelling of urine. I'd wet my pants in school or just off the bus at the end of my dreary days. It was embarrassing, really, to be potty-trained yet suddenly out-of-control of everything, including myself.

Ms. P seated me at one circular table all alone. It was the time-out table. I was already isolated due to my personality and new status, and the other kids sensed trouble: *something must be wrong with a student stuck constantly in the punishment area.* In the new kindergarten, I learned the words to "Feliz Navidad" and that you can't put green on a gingerbread man. Even my artwork was somehow wrong. Ms. P made classroom materials for everyone else but me. Months after I'd arrived, forgetting was no longer a legitimate excuse. I was smart enough to know that it didn't take more than fifteen seconds to write the name "Emily" in magic marker. So why did I have to decorate a paper plate craft that said "Tommy," yet Tommy didn't have one that said "Emily"?

There was a mystery, and I wanted to figure it out: what was I doing wrong to make the teacher treat me differently from the other kids? The year ended before I ever answered the question.

First grade was better, if only in comparison. Ms. F wasn't a very intellectually stimulating teacher, and I didn't connect with her, but at least she didn't hate my guts. It wasn't good enough, though—I already hated school. Each daybreak, as I prepared to leave the house, I was plagued by terrible stomachaches. I lost my shoes in various places around the house and cried from pain and anxiety. In the classroom, we began with "morning work," the fading purple-pixelated Xeroxed worksheets that repeated simple concepts ad nauseam. Every afternoon there was "D.E.A.R."—"drop everything and read"—but I usually wasn't allowed to read my chapter books. Instead, plastic dish-tubs of thin soft-covers must be read in order, according to their traffic light-coding. First came the easies, labeled with green tag-sale stickers along the spine, followed by the yellow-dotted mediums, before hard reds. To read a red book meant slogging through the dull greens and yellows first each day. Writing in the tan composition books was something I liked, but I wasn't quite sure why it was legal for anybody to mark up my *ideas* within the sacred space of my journal. Once we were allowed to write on big-kid lined paper, but my exuberant misuse of quotation marks in an experimental short story landed my creativity contained by red ink marks.

I didn't care for the other kids, and I was oblivious when they liked me. I didn't want playdates. I just wanted to hang out with my parents and siblings or recharge from the emotionally draining classroom. I spent one-third of my first-grade days absent. "She hasn't missed much," remarked Ms. F at a parent-teacher conference. My parents were worried. The teacher wasn't aware of the academic, social, and motor skills I missed or lacked because I was smart enough to pull by and quiet enough to melt into the background. My parents had me tested, and I qualified for a pull-out enrichment program once every ten days, but the school dragged its feet and said I was too young. My parents noted correctly that I needed help, but their meetings with the school got them nothing. The administrators and educators said I wasn't a big enough problem to help. Meanwhile, I spent recesses with my head on my desk and the lights out because one classmate had misbehaved so we all had to suffer. Listening to the lecture, I felt tremendous guilt. A bully tripped me in the classroom. I wet my overall shorts on the playground and left a pee puddle on the blacktop. We'd been waiting on line at the end of recess, but I was too frightened to say what I needed.

During story-time, Ms. F told us the news: instead of "looping," or staying our teacher for another year, she was going to marry a man named Mr. R and leave Pennsylvania. My classmates burst into eardrum-crushing chorus: *"Here comes the bride, all dressed in white, isn't she bee-eeeaautiful! Where is the groom? He's in the dressing room! Why is he there? He lost his underwear!"* I kept myself occupied counting how many students weren't singing with obnoxious loud voices—only four. Despite the raucous warning, Ms. F wanted her young scholars at her wedding. We sat with our parents in church pews with ninety-degree angles too sharp and puritanical for any human spine. Her wedding memory must be of two dozen sixes and sevens screaming "Ewwww!" as she frenched the love of her life.

She'd morphed into Mrs. R, a new person. The couple quietly moved away to California and on the first day of second grade, I had a nasty shock—Ms. P was standing by the chalkboard instead. She'd been assigned to the class of abandoned loopers. I was wary and upset, but starting the year alongside everybody else. With desks in pods of four, at least I couldn't be sequestered to the time-out table, and I knew where the bathroom was, so there was that. I was afraid of her, yet I desperately wanted her to like me. I drew her a picture as a present. "What is this ugly monster?" she jeered. Nothing had changed. My belly burnt with flames, and I spent hours sobbing and refusing to attend school or going and coming home a crumpled shadow of myself.

Everybody else loved Ms. P. The other parents had only nice things to say about her. My parents wanted to get to the bottom of things. Was the teacher really targeting me or were we all just being sensitive? They hired an independent counselor who validated the instinctual vibe that had left them searching for options: we were not insane, but the teacher, or at least her hideous behavior, most definitely was. The environment was toxic for me, and not just because I was allergic to the institutional carpeting and hand soap.

Besides the crying and refusing and anxiety and pain and boredom and complete ruin of self-esteem, my parents were concerned. Walking around the school halls with our hands behind our backs made their rule-bound child distressingly different even at home. I walked around our house with a more-serious-than-usual face, my hands clenched behind my back automatically.

First trimester of second grade, it was my turn to be Star Student. I was giving it a shot. I had my poster with pasted family photos and drawing and writing. For a shy withdrawn kid like me, this might as well have been the State of the Union Address. The day I was Star Student, my mom drove me in the silver minivan. Families could watch their Stars. We rounded the curve by the horse farm when—*Thud! Thud! Thud!*—we heard an unmistakable thunking noise and felt the car develop a lopsided gait, much like a horse with one lame leg.

It was a flat tire. We were stranded at the country roadside, and I was becoming highly late. My mother assured me it would all be okay, and it should have been. After we arrived, she explained the flat to an unsympathetic set of ears. Ms. P stood in front of the class, tall and menacing. She informed me in no uncertain terms that I'd need to give my presentation right then and there. I was overwhelmed with no time to calm myself down.

"Can she stay?"

"No," Ms. P said. "Your mom has to leave."

All the other children had their parents stay and watch! I was furious but without recourse. As she forced them to go, my tears could not be restrained and ran from my eyes like mustangs. I bawled.

"Stop crying, or I'll send you to the principal's office!" demanded the woman at the front of the room. Mr. T was a fine principal but everyone knew only people in big trouble went to see him. I had lost the ability to speak up for myself, so I knew I'd end up worse off there.

So I stood in front of my classroom, knobbly-kneed and blond-braided, my cheeks striped with salty tear-trails as new ones sprung from my eyes, and I was the Star Student. I was the Star Student just like that, sharing my life with conspicuously absent parent, my sole support forcibly removed, my speech about myself delivered to strangers through broken, wounded cries.

All this time, I knew I had done something wrong. I wasn't aware until later that my crime, according to Mrs. P, was simple: I existed. My parents pulled me out of school later that year, the day after a field trip to the New Jersey Aquarium. On the school bus ride there, I saw a car enveloped in explosive flames. At the aquarium, I saw a fish with four eyes: two looking for predators above the water, two below looking for predators in its midst. I identified with the fish, and it interested me. Under all the bullied ashamed feelings and unresolved issues, I was still a curious child who wanted to learn.

Necessity turned my mom and dad to alternative education. I was homeschooled for the next eight years, and it saved me. At home, my parents sparked my interests and helped me process the hurtful experiences I'd had in that school. My mom met my special needs and built up my confidence, countered my weaknesses, and fostered my talents. I am thankful that they took that leap.

When I reentered the system in high school, I realized how little had changed. There was still, in late teenage years, time wasted with morning work and the potential for red marks on my creative writing if I didn't include four metaphors—no more, no less. There were still confusing social situations, two-faced administrators, "right" and "wrong" ways to make artwork and interpret poetry, bullies, loud fire drills, anxiety, disconnect with classmates, boredom, stomachaches in the morning, tears, missed school buses, and nearly enough absences and tardiness to threaten me with losing credit. But I was okay. I think I was okay because I had the support, love of learning, and coping mechanisms I'd learned from my longest and best teachers, my parents.

Now I'm an adult who works with kids—and many of the kids are similar to me, kids with anxiety disorders, autism spectrum disorders, sensory processing disorders, and other disabilities. I've been an assistant teacher in traditional classrooms, and I've been an independent alternative educator facilitating classes and groups. My distressing elementary school experiences are often on my mind. They guide some of my decisions with children on a subconscious level. It's not just about loathing "Feliz Navidad" or the occasional pangs of insecurity that arise when I'm transported back to the countryside school. Just as my parents showed me through their actions how to teach kids in a good way, Ms. P showed me what I never wanted to be. I can recognize behavior like hers and stay strong. When former teaching colleagues began treating a few students in the classroom as Ms. P had treated me, I knew it was time to stand up and walk out of that environment, and I did. When a mom I know told me stories about a teacher who was eerily similar to Ms. P, I encouraged her to remove her child from the classroom and she did; she ended up finding a better fit for the child, who is now thriving instead of depressed and angry.

It'd be a corny yet devastating lie to say that I'm glad I had Ms. P as a teacher or thankful for what she taught me—it was painful, and I wish things had been different. Most of the time I try to forget she even existed. But because I had to go through that, I'm also hyper-aware of the positive or negative impact I can make on the children with whom I work. I stay conscious of my actions, especially of my mistakes. I look for ways to do a better job with the kids. When I teach kids and play with kids and support kids today, I see them as little humans who deserve respect and enjoy exploring when given enough of a chance.

I don't ever want to replicate my experience of the school system because that system was broken. Working through alternative education does give me freedom that some educators don't have, yet some attitudes I want to counter can be seen in any type of school. When I create a learning environment for kids, even if I don't mesh with a child, I have to know that my disconnect with this child cannot get in the way of treating him or her with the utmost respect. I will peak his interest, be on her team, set reasonable limits but encourage creativity. I create opportunities for each and every student to learn through play. They all have the freedom to fail.

Kids, especially those with mental health issues, neurological and learning disorders, and disabilities, need adults who believe in them and help them grow into themselves. I get tired of seeing the neediest students turn from happy, excited learners to unhappy institutional prisoners. It happens because they are set up to fail. Far too often, the worst treated are those with special needs—undiagnosed or diagnosed, visible or, like mine, invisible.

The only way to bring justice to education is to turn the focus to instilling love of learning in the very kids who have the most difficulty with learning. Let's restructure environments into spaces for success, provide encouragement, and preserve dignity, and kids won't have to suffer through power-struggle presentations and teacher torment to know they are Star Students.

TWENTY-TWO

Equations

By Cathleen Cohen

For my students

Karim won't read equations,
just tears pages in his binder.
He is angry at God,
who has grown incomprehensible,
striking trees, drying rains
before they reach their streams.

Last week two boys held his flailing arms
and a third one punched.
Scurry of legs, slammed lockers,
no teacher, fractured air,
he on the cold floor.

His parents speak of it
in careful English to the principal,
in Urdu laments at home.
No one says *racial*, but God subtracts,
abandoning his creatures.

At the mosque he won't pray,
only slumps on a wall.
Soon he will refuse to go
though his father shouts,
his mother weeps into her scarves.

It's not the red words hissing

through halls, through air,
but what he's learned of the deer
at water's edge, ears cocked
for any small click.

TWENTY-THREE

looking in the mirror in elementary school

By Sidrah Maysoon

i still tried to be beautiful
even though i was taught i was ugly
surrounded by white faces deemed ideal

in junior kindergarten, a girl
wouldn't play *stella ella ola* with me because she said
my hands were dirty and brown

i still tried to be beautiful
wearing fancy, colourful *hijabs*
trying to smile big enough to cover
my covered hair

a teacher in grade 6 told me
to get up and explain my religion to the class
because i was the only one wearing

sweat

i still tried to be beautiful
by excelling and starving myself

kids called me paki in grade 1 and beat us up
i found more violence at home
under every unturned stone
as i tried to be beautiful

by working hard

a workshop in grade 5 taught us that it was more difficult to be
a visible minority *and* a female at the same time
rather than just one or the other
i felt my skin burn
i smiled even bigger

what does trying to be beautiful have to do with it, you ask
with being in a classroom
with learning
with success

nothing, i answer
and smile

sweating

TWENTY-FOUR

The Tower, the Book, and the Girl They Let In

A Fable on Blackness and Racial Equity in the Academy

By Shannon Gibney

I.

There is a place, a time, a door, and a book. The girl with the brown hands opens the book, and while turning the pages, realizes that there is a thing called color and a thing called contrast, and that her hand is only brown when placed against the light blue of the book cover. As she reads on about cows and milking, high teas and delicate plum tarts, she realizes a thing called culture, although she does not yet have the word. There are fields in the book and there are factories, and the girl would like to think that were she there, she would play the part of the heroine.

The door slams suddenly, announcing dusk. This startles the girl, but she simply slumps deeper into the dank corner she has occupied for hours in the ancient university library. Safety in reams and reams of rotting old paper. The accumulation of thousands, millions of words finally coming to something more than itself.

This is her time. Her place. Her door. Her book.

When she stands up, she is thirty-six, with crumpled paper in her right hand, a stubbed pencil in her left. There was something she wanted to say: a story she was telling her students? A whisper of an image. That girl behind her who fell away, who believed in the story, was going to bring it into existence. The book sits on the floor half-opened, half-read. She doesn't want to know what it demands.

The time was too short.

73

Doors shutting all through the library. The building shivering.

What was it that she had wanted to do here, at the university? In 1983, in 2012? Her eyes open in alarm. The roar is deafening. It is a freight train clacking through the too-small stacks. The books fall in on themselves, the words go back.

Then this.

II.

Dear Shannon,

I am writing this letter to inform you of the results of the investigation into a complaint of racial harassment that was filed against you.

As you are aware, a student filed a complaint alleging that you engaged in conduct that was harassing toward him as a White male. He further alleged that you violated his privacy rights by disclosing an email message he sent to you to others who had no right to have this information. Pursuant to college policy, I am the decision-maker in this matter.

Sincerely,

Sincerely

III.

I have tried to tell this story many times. The problem is that the story keeps proliferating, so that I just end up asking myself where to invent a beginning. Should I begin with that fateful day six years ago, when the "powers that be" elected me worthy enough to take a position at the mid-sized public college in the Midwest where I teach? Should I begin with the first investigation? The second? Or with the formal review by a superior who castigated me for my approach to addressing racial equity and student success at the college? Perhaps I should begin with the moment my great-great grandfather picked up a chapter book and decided he would read it, cover to cover, even if the words sounded unintelligible to him. If I do start to unravel this long, braided story, will I ever end?

IV.

February, 2XXX

Okay, folks, here it is: My way of processing what has been going on with me these past few weeks.

I am sharing this with you because I love you, and I trust you to help me work through this traumatic experience without internalizing it.

I would love to hear your thoughts and comments on it, but as I stated at the beginning of the draft, please *DO NOT* print this out, forward it, or share it with anyone else: THIS IS FOR YOUR EYES ONLY. I tried to make information and individuals as general as possible, to get at the most important truths of the matter, but I am sure that the legal establishment could still find a way to misconstrue this.

Love,

Shan

"Waiting"

I am waiting for a letter to arrive in the mail. It will be short; no more than one page, printed in black ink, with the institutional logo. The signature at the bottom will belong to a high-ranking officer at my Midwestern college of twelve thousand students. The words that preface it will briefly explain the method and, more importantly, the verdict, of an almost three-week long investigation in which students, faculty, and staff were questioned by the school's legal staff as to whether, in fact, I had committed acts constituting an official case of racial harassment.

What happened to me recently did not happen because I am a young, Black, female faculty member at a school with over 50 percent students of color. What happened to me occurred because I magically turned the world backward on an angry White male student, and his knees started to crumble beneath him.

We were in a regular weekly meeting of the newspaper staff, and the students were discussing the most recent edition, how well it had turned out, and the editor-in-chief said that although he was proud of the paper's developments, he was not pleased with the fact that so few students regularly picked up the publication. It sat languishing on newsstands for weeks until the next edition was printed and took its place. Theories were thrown around as to why this was: the aesthetics were all wrong, the design didn't pop, and the stories could be flashier.

Another White male student, angry that writers had not made deadline, had thought it prudent to make a noose of his sweatshirt drawstring the fall before, to step up on the table and hang it, along with a menacing note to writers about the seriousness of deadlines. The two Black students in the room at the time had protested and asked him to take the noose down, but he didn't listen. When they told the faculty newspaper adviser of the incident, he told them that it was not such a big deal, that the student had not meant the noose in a racist way. And when the students finally filed a formal legal complaint against their colleague, seeking some kind of institutional acknowledgement of this trauma, they were effectively gagged by the same academic powers that have been conducting the investigation. You see, once language enters the legal realm, it no longer belongs to us; it becomes the property of whatever individual or institution is under its employ. (In fact, as I write these words now, fire burns under the fingertips of each key I strike. I know you feel their heat, their danger. I could be punished for saying this; I could lose my job because of these words.)

History has a bad habit of reappearing when we are least ready to see it, but the fleeting image of that noose would not leave my brain in that newsroom meeting. Nor could the conflagration of so many White bodies in one space (the entire editorial staff except for one Somali student who I had brought to the meeting from my Newspaper Activity class), while so many brown ones clustered outside it, largely indifferent to its power, but also wounded from the violence that had taken place there, the wiping away of voices. *I think this staff needs to deal with the fact that this newsroom, and the newspaper in general, has historically been a space where White male experience has been centralized and validated, mostly to the exclusion of all others*, I said. *That is the elephant in the room, the thing that no one wants to talk about, but your readership will continue to flag in a school that is more than half students of color if the editorial staff continues to not represent their interests. In short, they don't see themselves in the paper because they* are not *in the paper*, I said.

Silence.

The clock ticked.

Eyes rolled.

And I received an email, full of roiling, angry emotion from a White male editor later that night. He said that my words had angered him, that it wasn't my place to say them, being a faculty member in the student newsroom. He said that my comments were racist and hateful, that they were akin to a White man standing up and saying that all Black women were irrational, and that my understanding of race was facile if I thought that White people was actually a tenable category. He said that I would not be welcome in the newsroom in the future if I offered up a similar diatribe, and that I had engaged in racial harassment.

In the dark upstairs of my study at 10:32 p.m. my breath shallowed. I checked the windows to make sure they were locked, closed my eyes and began to count to twenty slowly. The thing is, I was never supposed to be there; these institutions were not built for Black women, or for anyone of color, to live or work in. In fact, they were built to keep us *out.* I know this intellectually, being a student of history, but every time I come up against the blunt-end truth of it, I still shiver. It is an emotion for which I still can't seem to find a home. But his message still demanded a response— ideally one that was as dispassionate as his was emotional. Ida B. Wells, Fannie Lou Hamer, Harriet Jacobs, were my predecessors, racially, culturally, but most importantly, politically. I knew who had brought me to this place.

Writing back, I thanked the student for bringing the issue to my attention, and said that certain faculty and students had been discussing the future of the student newspaper and the future of the journalism program itself for some time, and that the entire school community would have to weigh in on it in order to come to a viable solution. I said that I was carbon copying his message and my response to those individuals already engaged in this conversation, to further facilitate this interaction. I repeated my earlier statements about the history of the newsroom and newspaper itself being an unwelcome place for people of color, and said that last year's noose incident was just the most recent demonstration of this inequity. I reminded him that our school was over 50 percent students of color and that any organization that did not make a concerted effort to include them would therefore not succeed. Finally, I urged him to educate himself about the history of race and White privilege in this country, and invited him to an all-campus event that a colleague and I were invited to host on this topic later that week.

The student must have forwarded my message to the general newspaper account, because another editor, a young White woman, wrote back. She said that I had completely missed the point of the first student's email, and echoed his characterization of my comments at the meeting as being racist and hurtful. Our door is open to all, she wrote, and demanded an apology. I felt my blood heat up and I forced myself to breathe slowly while I counted to twenty again. *I find it more than a little shocking that you all believe that I am the one who must make an apology,* I wrote. *I have never received an email as threatening and blatantly disrespectful, and I find it quite troubling that the only Black faculty member that has ever been associated with the journalism program is now being accused of racial harassment.* I ended my message by endorsing the newspaper adviser's idea for mediation. The student wrote back that he found my second response even more perverse than the first, and had been advised to consult a higher power, and quoted the school's racial harassment policy. *Do not have any further contact with him,* colleagues advised. *Your words can, and probably will, be used against you.*

I had been trying to restructure the conversation from one about individuals to one about systems and structures, and he had been resisting from the start. It was an interesting irony that his tactic of accessing the legal establishment was, in fact, a way to abandon the narrative of the individual, and tap into the power of the institution which, like all American institutions, was indelibly forged out of disciplining the racialized, gendered, lower-class masses. Once he did that, the story was as predictable as a Harlequin Romance novel. The form was overdetermined from the start. I had seen this, but it is like encountering a traffic jam on your way home from work: you know there is no other way home, so you just have to continue on.

The next week, a member of the college leadership interviewed me for an hour, grilling me with questions about what I had said when, to whom, and what my email messages had contained, who they were sent to, and why. This person also interviewed the newspaper adviser, several other student editors, and staff members who had been there. It was all fairly terrifying.

Perhaps I shouldn't have spoken. The words crowded in my mind on more than one occasion when, during the three-week interview process, I awoke at 5 a.m., my thoughts running around the room in circles. But then I heard the voice of the young Somali student in my class, who would have to attend the remainder of the newspaper staff meetings without me because I was to have no contact with the student who filed the complaint while it was under investigation. The young woman, in her early twenties, had approached me at the start of the semester and mentioned that she didn't think that she should stay in my class because her English was not very good. I had replied that the purpose of a writing class was to work on your writing, and that therefore she was in the right place. But that afternoon, when I told the class that I would no longer be attending newspaper staff meetings with them because of what they had all heard me say the week before, the young woman protested. *But what you said was true! When I walked into that first meeting and saw that it was all White people, no one who looked like me, I wanted to walk away.* What was left unsaid was, *But I didn't.* I wondered, I still wonder, what had made her stay. The next week, when I saw her in the hallway before she left for the staff meeting, she revealed that she did not want to go. I could see the fear in her eyes, visceral, and too familiar. I told her that she could leave and come up to the classroom at any time if she found that she could not stay. She nodded, and turned toward the stairwell. I hoped she would stay in the meeting and keep writing her stories, but I also was prepared for her to have to leave. You can only be alone for so long before your own clothes start to feel strange on your body.

But now I am still waiting. Waiting for the letter to arrive. Waiting for an answer to questions no one wants to ask.

The letter.

The silence.

The ripping open. At the thought of it, my heart jumps in my throat.

V.

February 2XXX

Dear Shannon,

After careful consideration of all the information presented to me, I have concluded that your conduct did not rise to the level of the college's nondiscrimination policy. However, while I find that your conduct did not meet the policy standards of discriminatory harassment, I hope that you are able to understand that your comments were offensive to the complainant and to others and inappropriately made during the newspaper staff meeting.

Sincerely,

Sincerely

VI.

Her face.

Bright eyes shining a light lit long ago, raised by immigrant parents who gave her everything they never had in Haiti but thought she needed to be okay so she wouldn't have to make sixty beds a morning and clean up other people's fingernails and toilet paper and mucous. Somehow, she and I both ended up here, at this college. We keep each other together. And there's the White woman who won't look away and never stops fighting and the Sister from Chicago who wasn't supposed to be let in here either, and the Asian American woman whom they mistake as a "Model Minority," but who has never aligned herself politically with White, middle-class folks.

These are the four small pieces of matter that keep me in the orbit of this college; they, and our generous, overburdened, challenged, hard-working students. Otherwise I would fall off, a piece of debris floating in the dead freeze of space.

Perhaps I would be better off, healthier. But would my students?

VII.

As we proceed, I would caution Professor Gibney to understand that whatever message she may be motivated to share with her department and the college as a whole, the "delivery mode" is as important as the message itself: the ability to cooperate well with others will go a long way toward moving the institution forward on the issues of primary import. The issue, then, is the definition of "cooperation." If cooperation implies a kind of stated or unstated agreement with the status quo, then I cannot agree to "cooperate" with the members of my department and college, who are predominantly White and upper-middle class, who come from families with a history of college success, and who have absolutely no awareness of their own privilege and how it might impact their interactions with and expectations of students, many of whom are brown, working class, and first-generation college students. This kind of "cooperation" has only yielded a 7 percent completion rate for our Black male students and a 12 percent completion rate for Black female students, when students of African descent comprise 33 percent of our population. In this context, cooperation should be recognized as contributing to educational failure for the majority of people whose money we take while we claim to serve them.

Closing the achievement gap at the college is, to my mind, one facet of racial justice. Collegial relations are central to this endeavor. When has upholding the importance of collegial relations in all interactions with the powerful ever worked to the benefit of the oppressed? Trying our very best to get along with White folks and not make them uncomfortable has not been a very successful strategy in order to address the persistent so-called racial "achievement gap" in this state, which continues to be the biggest in the country.

We all need members of the faculty to find common cause around this issue and to participate fully within the boundaries set by community etiquette and the shared desire for a genuine and free exchange of ideas working toward concrete and student-centered solutions. Unfortunately, what I have experienced here is that the vast majority of faculty and administrators have no investment in finding common cause around racial equity. In fact, I would say that the majority of them may fear racial equity because embracing it would mean that they would have to radically change their pedagogies, course curricula, policies, and—and this is the real rub, I think—the racial and ethnic make-up of the faculty and leadership, which is still more than 90 percent White.

Professor Gibney's passion to find racial justice for our students needs to be part of our work here at the college. But how can I do that when finding racial justice for our students is not part of our work at the college? One could argue persuasively that, economically, the college is set up to benefit from the lack of racial justice here.

It is my hope that she will get up to speed in the academic year and contribute to these efforts in a positive, cooperative, and productive manner. There are few adjectives that can fuel such enmity in me. I am not the one whose behavior needs to be examined, whose message is faulty, or whose positivity conceals a very thin layer of contempt.

VIII.

"White people know that all over the world people of color have been brutally and unjustly treated by white imperialism. White people know how violent they have been to each other and to us and they know our grievances are real; and thus they imagine how much more violent we would be to them, with our *real* history of violations. This is why every demand for respect and recognition of dignity on our part is read as a sign of violence. This is why white people so fear black people in the United States, despite the fact that it is white people who have a history of violence against black people and not the other way around."

—Haunani-Kay Trask, "The Politics of Academic Freedom as the Politics of White Racism"

IX.

March 2XXX

Dear Shannon,

I am writing regarding the complaint of race and gender discrimination that was filed against you in December 2XXX by a former temporary faculty member.

The complainant alleged that he had been subjected to harassment and discriminatory treatment based on his race and gender. In particular, the complainant alleged that the English Department's requirement of critical race theory as a preferred hiring qualification discriminated against him as a White male. The complainant also alleged that the English Department generally promoted a hostile or discriminatory environment for White males based on the actions of a few faculty members who promoted critical race and White privilege theories.

After carefully considering all relevant information, I have determined that the evidence is insufficient to conclude that you engaged in conduct that violated the Nondiscrimination Policy. Despite this finding, I have asked X to review the hiring preferences and to explore preferences that would ensure a broad and inclusive pool of qualified candidates. I am concerned that identifying a preference to a specific theory may result in excluding qualified candidates who may be able to demonstrate their commitment to diversity in other ways.

Sincerely,

Sincerely

X.

"All three investigations triggered by my column have been concluded in my favor: nothing I did was worthy of reprimand or removal.

But the message of all this investigating is simply this: if, in a public forum, faculty members of color exercise the right to argue a position that is contrary to, and critical of, white ideology, they will be investigated. Moves by white faculty or white students against people of color will be protected, however." —Haunani-Kay Trask, "The Politics of Academic Freedom as the Politics of White Racism"

XI.

Why did they let her in, if just to spit her out as they engulfed her?

The book still spoke to her sometimes, but the story was elusive, the words rattled. There was no passion but misplaced passion, and not enough bandages to mend the busted doors.

In the end, she didn't mind reading the story from the back of her hands. She knew it well enough anyway, carrying it in her thighs, her hair, her shoulders all these years, and her cell structures all these centuries. But who would listen?

The people: the people needed the story as much as she did. But they had never even heard of the book.

TWENTY-FIVE

To Lumpia or to Not Lumpia?

*A Counterstory of a Multicultural Racial
Microaggression*

By Cheryl E. Matias

The excitement was on. Only a few days before the school-wide first-ever Multicultural Food Fair. "What are you bringing?" cried every student on campus. Teachers were frazzled with organizing parades, information cards, and national flags that will decorate the once droning red brick hallways. Parents were hustling and bustling trying to grab traditional family recipes and storming local grocery marts. The school and the community were abuzz. What a spectacle it will be.

I was no different for I have waited five years to finally share my Filipino cultural food. Along with my younger sister, we made up the school's "Pacific Islander" category, and there was an immense pressure to represent this category with full valor. Each night my sister, Heidi (a.k.a. Hides), and I went home discussing the possible Filipino food for the day's extravaganza. It had to be something delicious, attractive, and accessible.

"What about Adobo?" suggested Heidi.

"Hell no, Hides. Don't get me wrong. It's gooood. But it's ooogly. I don't want people thinkin' we eat ugly food." We sat there perplexed in silence as we brainstormed for more ideas. With a laugh I said, "Maybe we should bring them Dinaguan." *A very unattractive dish which uses pig's blood.* Both of us crackled over the idea.

"Hides, I got it! We'll bring Lumpia and the sweet and sour sauce. It's good, attractive, and easy to eat. We'll be a hit!" Heidi agreed and we pounced off our bed dashing straight to our mom to relay our choice.

***

My sister and I woke up extra early on the day of the Multicultural Food Fair to have time to make sure we looked snazzy. I put on my favorite jeans, multicolored shirt, and topped it off with a beautifully glittered jean jacket. My sister was equally dashing in her purple overalls and hand-me-down Rainbow Bright T-shirt. I checked my bag for our index card that neatly and clearly labeled our dish as "LUMPIA—A Filipino Dish." I smiled proudly as my sister and I reread our short information card that discussed the geography of the Philippines, the cultural heritage, and a brief description of the ingredients for Lumpia. We were impressed and beyond satisfied with our efforts and passion that was put into our presentation of Lumpia. I carefully grabbed the perfectly wrapped dish and slowly brought it down from the counter. Then Heidi and I made our way to the bus.

After what seemed like an eternity on the bus, we dismounted and arrived at our "booth." Then we began the painstaking process of arranging our dish in our rehearsed precision mode. Heidi grabbed the Filipino Flag and taped it onto the edge of the desk. I started to put our map of the Philippines for our background. Then, together, we ever so carefully positioned the dish of Lumpia on the table while gently removing the wrapping. I set the sweet-and-sour sauce right next to the Lumpia. It was finally time to display the two index cards. I affixed the "LUMPIA—A Filipino Dish" card directly below the elevated dish. Heidi put the information card directly below the sweet-and-sour-sauce container. We were finally done. A picture of perfection. Without a doubt I knew our table was the featured attraction of the Multicultural Food Fair. Feeling assured, Heidi and I went to the restroom to relieve our liquid nervousness.

"We did it, Ate Cheryl. Ours is the best out there," exclaimed Heidi as we made our way back to our table to once again check on our prized possession. "I think you're right, Hides." I assured her. We reached our destination and to our surprise someone had changed it. In place of our "Lumpia—A Filipino Dish" card was a card that sloppily read "EGGROLLS." Shocked by the deliberate cultural sabotage I grabbed the card and together we ran to my teacher to tattle on suspected fellow classmates. "Mrs. Pekuri! Something terrible has happened!" Mrs. Pekuri turned around and smiled a patronizing smile down at us. "Yes, girls. What's wrong?"

"Mrs. Pekuri, someone changed our title card from Lumpia to Eggroll." Mrs. Pekuri chuckled a bit. She looked at Heidi then to me while firmly shaking her head in disbelief.

"Sweethearts, I changed it. People won't understand what Lumpia is so it's best we identify it as eggrolls. That way people will know what it is." Heidi and I looked at each other, and I clearly saw the formation of tears in the corner of her eyes. She turned around and ran to the bathroom. I turned back to Mrs. Pekuri, who was already off helping decorate Vicky's Irish Potato Salad exhibit. I ran after Heidi to the restroom and there, we both hunched in the corner and through our tears I whispered, "No matter what she says or anybody else, we know it's Lumpia. We know, Hides. We know."

TWENTY-SIX

The New Girl

By Sheila O'Connor

The new girl smells like gone. Lost things. Like dirty clothes and cigarettes and cats. She smells like the last place where she lived, apartment 303, in Newport, ceiling cracks, and cockroaches. The place where she kept her brother in her bed, where they went hungry, so she stole a bag of Fritos from the QuikTrip, and got caught. The new girl smells like stealing. She's arrived without supplies. No paper, no pencil, no calculator for math class. No folder, no eraser. Everything she's missing makes the teacher hate her more. She should know the things she needs at a new school. They can't run a charity. She's come without $2.50 for a lunch. Did she think they would just feed her? No, the new girl says, she isn't hungry. The new girl stands alone in line. She stands alone at recess. She smells like sticky hands and sweat, like a piggy bank that's empty, coppery and dirty. She smells like pennies. She smells like movies she didn't see, like the slumber party stories she can't tell. She smells like the desk at the last school she left. The watermelon scratch-and-sniff eraser, the little monkey doodles she drew when she was bored. The tiny folded note left in her jacket. RAG. She smells like jokes. She smells like lice and cooties, like B.O. and gross. Trash. White trash. She smells like questions she can't answer: Who shows up at school with nothing? The new girl smells like grease, like the truck stop where she brushed her teeth this morning. She smells like bags in the backseat, and everything they owned sacked-up like garbage. She smells like garbage. She smells like rotting apples and the rent they never paid. The new girl smells like owing. She smells like someone running, like someone panting, like someone who's been begging since the day she was born.

Section Questions: Being the Target

1. In this section, there are many examples of people being bullied, from students to college professors. List the reasons for bullying. What do you see in your life that lets the bullies take over? How can this be changed?

2. In the works by Shannon Gibney, Sidrah Maysoon, and Cathleen Cohen, racism plays a central role in being a target. Discover the ways this plays out in each piece. What is needed to change white supremacy in each of these pieces?

3. In "The New Girl" by Sheila O'Connor, she describes in one page all the ways a child is targeted to feel shame. Describe times you have seen targeting and what you did or did not do. What part does silence play in the experiences of those in this section. What part does timidity play?

Part V

Claiming Our Space and Identities

We can spend our lives letting the world tell us who we are. Sane or insane. Saints or sex addicts. Heroes or victims. Letting history tell us how good or bad we are. Letting our past decide our future. Or we can decide for ourselves. And maybe it's our job to invent something better.
—Chuck Palahniuk, *Choke*

If you're white and you're wrong, then you're wrong; if you're black and you're wrong, you're wrong. People are people. Black, blue, pink, green—God make no rules about color; only society make rules where my people suffer, and that why we must have redemption and redemption now.
—Bob Marley

Words are power. The more words you know and can recognize, use, define, understand, the more power you will have as a human being . . . The more language you know, the more likely it is that no one can get over on you.
—Quraysh Ali Lansana and Georgia A. Popoff (selection from book: *Our Difficult Sunlight: A Guide to Poetry, Literacy and Social Justice in Classroom and Community*)

Perhaps finding out that we carry New World history in our genes will transcend racial checkboxes altogether and enable Latino-Americans to rethink what America is supposed to look like.
—Raquel Cepeda, *Birds of Paradise: How I Became Latina*

If what I read doesn't reflect my life—whether I'm gay or Latino or on welfare—doesn't that really mean that my life is not valuable?
—Walter Dean Myers

TWENTY-SEVEN

White Hallways

By Cora-Lee Conway

white hallways,
and white floors.
white ceilings,
and white doors.
white clocks with black hands telling white time,
blackboards affixed to chalk white lines,
white teachers to tell white history,
where are the teachers that look like me?
black janitor to clean white mess
black mothers to hear black girls' distress
They say I'm not pretty, they say I'm not clean,
They tell me I'm not smart. I know they're being mean
white girls with long hair
white privilege does not care
black girls in white schools
'educated' to make smart a fool
color bound, twice removed
disavowed and unapproved
talking back is not condoned
silence deep like treasures owned
but kinships across time and space
insist that resistance can't be replaced
at the site where you are truly embraced
race erased to make space for that sweet face
laced like trebled notes over that low bass
spoken slow
you make no haste
deliberate and bold

there is no mistake
you take
white hallways
to burst through
white doors
crash through
white ceilings
glide over
white floors
black girls move like rag-time
rightfully inclined to redefine the line
take your spotlight, rise and shine

TWENTY-EIGHT

First Generation College Blues

By Rosanna M. Salcedo

The room smelled of varnished wood and moth-eaten books. I knew why I had been called to the office, but I wondered why had I agreed to come to this small, prestigious, liberal arts college. In the stillness of the room, I could hear the ticking of the grand, old clock. It had a shiny plaque I could not read from where I sat. I imagined the words—*A gift from the class of 1954*—inscribed on it, or some such thing. A large, porcelain bowl sat on a polished mahogany coffee table. It was imprinted with dusty rose etchings of one of the original campus buildings, dating back to the 1820s. It would never be used as a receptacle for anything, it was not meant to be useful, it was meant to be symbolic—a symbol of things achieved, of tradition, and membership—a trophy, perhaps. The carved details on the fireplace mantle, the upholstered furniture, the heavy drapes, the incredibly detailed woolen rugs that protected the shiny hardwood floors, all of it suggested wealth and privilege, a world I read about in novels, saw in movies, and had imagined. Now I was a part of it, but not really. Feeling like a rude guest in someone else's home, I stopped exploring the room with my eyes and relaxed my grip on the arms of the chair.

The academic dean was sitting behind the desk reading my file. We hadn't made eye contact yet, and that was fine. I didn't want him to look at me. I was already feeling ashamed, and I was afraid of what I might see in his eyes—reproach, pity, indifference? This was a mistake. They had made a mistake.

The balding, middle-aged school administrator finally looked up. "Rosanna, it looks like you've been having some academic trouble."

95

He pronounced my name the way most White Americans do—nasally, so it rhymes with "banana." I much prefer the way my mother says it (Ros-ah-na), but at that moment, in that room, and under those circumstances, even if he had said my name just the way I like to hear it, it would have sounded harsh. I was ashamed to be there, and that he had to say my name at all.

"Last semester you failed calculus and earned a D in economics. We've allowed you to take calculus again this term so that you can fulfill the math requirement for graduation, but your professor reports that you're not doing much better."

I tried not to blink so the tears that had been pooling in my eyes would not spill over onto my face. I had never been in academic trouble before. This was not characteristic of me. This was not part of my profile, and it disturbed me. What does it mean that I'm doing poorly in school? Am I stupid? How did I make it this far? Had I fooled all my previous teachers? I was feeling resentment towards them now. They said I was smart. They said I could do this—that I have what it takes.

"How have you been addressing your difficulties in math, Rosanna?" He continued.

"I'm working with a peer tutor several times a week. I don't know . . . I don't know why . . . I'm just not getting it." I stammered, feeling embarrassed and apologetic.

"Well, that's good. I mean it's good that you're getting the extra help because you have to pass math to graduate. You also have to maintain a good academic record in general."

He didn't say I would be expelled, but we both knew that Amherst College would not tolerate a poor academic record for too long.

"Have you considered counseling?" he asked.

I felt my face get hot again, and my guts tighten. Yes, clearly, there was something wrong with me.

My counselor was a slender, middle-aged, white woman, with coiffed blond hair, natural-looking makeup, and shiny studs in her ears. She wore cable knit sweaters, tweed pants, and sensible, quality loafers—the kind of understated affluence that suggests upper-middle class New England. I imagined many of my peers at Amherst would look like her in twenty years. How could I explain to her what I was feeling, and how could she possibly understand? What could she possibly say that would make me feel better? It didn't matter, because she didn't ask me about my family, or what my life had been like back home. She was only interested in listing the strategies I should use to improve my academic performance.

"Yes, I'm seeing a counselor." I almost whispered.

"Good. Unfortunately, we're still going to have to put you on academic probation this semester. You have until the end of the year to bring up your grades."

I nodded, eyes downcast.

"Good luck, Rosanna."

That was it. That was the extent of our meeting. I walked out into the chill of early spring. There were still mounds of dirty snow here and there, in places where it had been piled during the last snowfall, but I could see little blades of grass, and crocuses, fighting to break through the frozen soil on some of the lawns. As I walked away from the hundred-year-old stone building, I felt like there still wasn't one adult in the entire place who knew me. None of the adults, not one, had taken any time to get to know me. Not even the counselor. I suppose, if I could have talked to my parents, things might have been better, but I couldn't talk to them about it either. There wasn't anyone I could talk to about what I was going through. I was the first generation in my family to attend college, and I was away from home. This was not something they could help me with, or understand. Sometimes, when I spoke to them on the phone, I couldn't keep myself from crying. They worried of course, and asked what was the matter, but I couldn't tell them the truth. I couldn't tell them that I was struggling, that it was too hard, that I was unhappy, because they might ask me to come home. I didn't want to come home— not really. I knew that I was doing something no one back home had done, and I did not want to fail. I didn't want to disappoint anyone, especially myself. So I told them I was a little homesick. That's all. No big deal.

I was so embarrassed about having been called into the Dean's office, I didn't want to talk about it with anyone, especially my peers, because I thought it would confirm what I believed they already suspected: that I didn't belong there, I wasn't smart enough, the admissions committee had made a mistake. I went back to my dorm room that afternoon, and said nothing to my roommates. They were nice girls. They would have expressed plenty of sympathy, and offered words of encouragement, but that would have hurt my pride even more.

My roommates were Lily and Sarah. Lily was a Chinese American, from Texas, and both of her parents had professional careers. They were architects or engineers. She played the guitar and became involved in an organization called Christian Fellowship on campus. She fell right in place. My other roommate, Sarah, was a Jewish American from California. Her mother was a university professor and her father a neurosurgeon. She loved music as well, and played the flute. She knew the soundtrack to *Les Misérables* by heart, and sang along every day while she did her work in our room. I didn't play an instrument, and I never played my music out loud, only through my earphones. I was afraid my Spanish music, or the popular rap and hip-hop to which I listened, would sound unsophisticated and I would be judged.

Sarah had an older brother who also attended the school, and he introduced her to his friends. I tagged along sometimes with Lily or

Sarah, and people were polite enough to me, but I couldn't relate much to what they talked about: their suburban high schools, tailgating parties, family vacations to tropical rain forests, summer camp experiences. I had nothing to contribute to these conversations, and I did not feel safe sharing stories of my own. I only listened, but if I had had the courage to share, this is what I would have said about what life was like at home:

I grew up in Washington Heights, New York City—a neighborhood of Latino immigrants, many of us undocumented. It was the kind of place where you could buy antibiotics from the pharmacist without a prescription and get your hard drugs at the *bodega*, but to me it was home, and I felt safe there. We shared the neighborhood with other immigrants: Eastern European Jews, Orthodox Greeks, and a splattering of Blacks and Asians from a variety of countries, but the majority were Latinos, particularly from the Dominican Republic, like my parents. If I walked east a few blocks from where I lived to St. Nicolas Avenue, I could haggle with unlicensed street vendors, their merchandise sprawled on the sidewalks, and purchase fresh *caña*, *agua de coco*, and *empanadas* from makeshift carts. *Merengue* blared from passing cars, open windows, and many storefronts where men gathered to play dominos on card tables. Little girls with multiple pigtails, fastened tightly with colorful elastics, followed their mothers, or maybe their sisters or their grandmothers. You couldn't tell generations apart sometimes. If you looked around, you could see every imaginable shade of brown.

My public elementary school was a K–8. I remember the metal grates that covered each of the windows, and the shiny gray paint that covered all the floors of the gray brick building. One of us discovered that if we rubbed the soles of our sneakers in just the right way it made a squeaky sound. Squeak! Squeak! Squeak! When the principal realized we were doing it intentionally, he threatened to keep all of us in at recess, so we stopped, because detention meant sitting at an empty lunch table in silence, instead of going outside. The schoolyard was a large rectangle, surrounded by a chain link fence at least thirty feet high, painted a cheerful blue. The fence was meant to keep us safe, and security guards stood by the entrance gate to make sure. The yard had a couple of net-less basketball hoops, and there were some jump ropes strewn about. That was the extent of the playground equipment. We were told to use our imaginations.

My brothers, friends, and I spoke Spanglish during recess, at home, and around the neighborhood. We adopted English words and pronounced them the way we heard them in Spanish: for breakfast we might eat *"Conflé co n leche"* (cornflakes with milk). We also switched from one language to the other seamlessly.

"I'm hungry. *Voy pa' la bodega* to buy some chips. *Tú quieres algo?*"

"No thanks, *mami* cooked *arroz con pollo*, I'm having dinner *en casa*."

Our teachers, all of whom were White and did not live in our neighborhood, didn't like it when we spoke this way. They gave us disapproving looks and told us to "speak English." We knew the difference. We spoke that way because we could, and they could not.

In the summer, in a good year, when my father received plenty of overtime, or did a lot of side jobs under the table, we might be able to visit our relatives in the Dominican Republic, and enjoy the beaches there. If we couldn't travel back to the island, we spent the summers playing in the street, or the local park, which was mostly paved in asphalt. One of the neighborhood men might use a wrench to loosen the nut on the fire hydrant, letting the water gush out, and the kids cool down. Or maybe, once or twice, in a New York City summer, we made the two-hour ride to Sunken Meadow State Park, to wade into the murky waters of the Long Island Sound. These are the things I could have said to my new college friends, but did not have the courage.

The fall of my freshman year I had to deal with my first Homecoming Weekend. The schedule of events for that weekend had been published: a meet and greet with the president of the college; several lectures on a variety of topics that would seem esoteric even to most college-educated people; performances by a number of a cappella groups; and of course, the Sunday afternoon football game against our equally privileged rival, Williams College. Dilemma: What would I do with my parents if they came? Who would they talk to? My parents didn't speak English, and they didn't know anything about American football. They couldn't afford to stay at a hotel. Should I have them drive four hours to see me, only to have dinner, and then drive four hours back? I tried to gauge their feelings about the topic, but the thought of their visit made me anxious. I told them they shouldn't make the long drive, and I had a lot of work to do.

"Don't worry about this weekend, Mami. It's not a big deal." I said, but the shame burned a hole is my stomach. They didn't come, and I did not go home. I saved the money to buy a bus ticket later in the fall to get home for the Thanksgiving break.

It was the beginning of the spring semester and I was still feeling lost, adrift. I was still struggling with calculus and economics—a class of about sixty men and four women. The four of us sat in the back row. When I looked around the room, I saw male, White faces almost exclusively, and I thought, "What am I doing here?" That class represented an even more drastic social and demographic reality. I listened passively to the professor, and interacted with very few of the students. I struggled, but I passed calculus and economics, and decided never to take another course in those respective departments again.

When it was time to choose courses for the next fall semester, I decided to explore other disciplines: Women and Gender Studies, Latin American History, Sociology, Psychology. I discovered that there was more diversity in these classes, and that I had some frame of reference for these subjects. I had something to contribute, and did not feel as out of place. Even though I still struggled with feelings of inferiority, I began to enjoy my classes more.

Things improved most dramatically in my third year at the college. I had taken a couple of psychology courses the previous year, and was becoming more and more interested in the subject. That year, Amherst hired a visiting professor to teach in the Psychology and African American Studies departments. Her name was Dr. Ira Blake, a Black woman, with a PhD. There were relatively few women teaching at the college, and even fewer women of color, perhaps not any. Professor Blake was only going to be there for a year, and after reading her bio, I decided I would enroll in a class with her for the fall and spring. Her interests lay in the intersection of psychology and education. I remember discussing things like: language acquisition, cultural styles of childrearing, and the impact of socioeconomic factors on the school-aged child. I saw myself reflected in some of the case studies we explored, and found I could provide the class with invaluable insight. Professor Blake met with me individually, and engaged me in conversations about my experiences. Her feedback on my papers was validating and encouraging. She helped me explore my interests and allowed me to tap into my strengths.

I began to look at my situation through a wider lens, not through the narrow eyelet focused on my personal suffering. I wasn't affluent, and I had not arrived at Amherst College with the cultural capital that most of the other students had, but I was still there, learning, making my way through the system, and excelling in my area of interest. If Ira Blake could stand before a class at Amherst, then maybe I did belong there, and I could aspire to do the same some day.

In the spring of my senior year, graduate-school acceptance letters poured in. I could have my pick, and settled for the Harvard Graduate School of Education. My parents drove up for graduation in their old Toyota station wagon, wearing their Sunday best. This time, I wanted them there, and as close to the front as possible. It didn't matter that they couldn't understand most of the words during the ceremony, as long as they could hear my name and see me walk across the stage.

TWENTY-NINE

Learning Up Front

By Curtis Robbins

For as long as I remember
I sat up front of the class
so I could watch Teacher
otherwise I'd be sitting
in the back somewhere
reading lips
between bobbing, swaying, nodding heads:
some were tall
some were fat
some had perms wide or high
some had bushy ducktails
some had crewcuts
the rest didn't matter

As long as I sat up front
so I could watch Teacher.

Some teachers
    talked chalk poking the blackboard
Some teachers
    talked flipping fanning pages
Some teachers
    talked zigzagging rows of aisles
    that bobbing, swaying, nodding
    heads didn't matter

As long as I sat up front
    so I could watch Teacher.

When my classmates spoke
    I never knew
    as long as I sat up front
    so I could watch Teacher.

Whether meticulous notes were
    written on the blackboard or
    on blue on white
    nauseating ammonized ditto or
    on black on white
    ink-blotted, letter-smudged
    mimeograph or

    read from the book

As long as I sat up front
    so I could watch Teacher.

Never once could I tell
how much I understood—
a day never went
without daydreams—
it never really mattered
as long as I sat up front
so I could watch Teacher.

THIRTY

The Way I Am

By Min Feldman

You see
An outcast
I see
One of a kind

You see
Charcoal face
I see
Chocolate skin

You see
Weird
I see
Beautiful

THIRTY-ONE

Independence Day

By Elizabeth L. Sammons

By the summer I was eight, most families who owned Victorian homes were already spending time and money to decorate and restore their houses for the bicentennial. Even two years ahead of time, Main Street in Mount Vernon, Ohio boasted freshly planted trees on both sides, while everywhere, it seemed, liberty bells, flags, and Spirit of 76 banners already waved from porch pillars. At least, my parents told me so; being blind, I was unable to see these details for myself.

That summer of 1974, my parents hired a lawyer for $1 to help them convince the powers that be in our local school system that it was time for them to mainstream their first child with a disability. Among conditions laid down was a decision that I would not attend school in my own district, but that I needed to go to the only one-story school in town, and, I should add, the only school with a male fifth-grade teacher. To go to that school, however, I would need to take a bus. This bus would not come to my house, but to the school within my own district several blocks away. Looking back, I think that the authorities wanted to intimidate my family by making them concerned for my need to cross a number of streets to get to the bus stop. Obviously they did not know us very well.

My parents agreed to the conditions. They began trying to make me use a white cane when I went more than one block away from our house.

It is difficult for me to convey the impact of that ultimatum. While I had my share of childhood bumps and bruises, doubtless some of which were due to my low vision, I never wanted to use a cane. In my eight-year-old mind, the cane meant shouting to the world that I was blind and needed special care from adults. As for the children I wanted to impress, the cane was just inviting special ridicule. I can remember holding the cane stiffly in front of me, refusing to let its tip touch the ground. After watching me, my parents told me that if I did not learn to use a cane properly, I could not attend schools in my hometown as I wanted to, because I was creating danger for myself and others. A policeman, my mother told me, would be coming in a week, and he would be walking with me from my house to the bus stop. As a neutral party agreed on by the town and my parents, this policeman would decide whether or not I was a community hazard.

I thought this over for about ten minutes, after which I told my parents I had decided that two hours a day commuting to a blind class in another town was not worth the price of not learning to use my cane. I was angry, but I knew I had to learn something the right way. I began to let my hand and arm relax and become flexible. Then I discovered what my hard-tipped cane could show me as it tapped the ground, bumped tree root swells, slid along and cracks between bricks in the street, or jumped from sidewalk to curb.

When the policeman came to our door, I was ready. While I was walking with him, I asked him "What do you think about the bicentennial?" He answered, "Everybody is supposed to be free." And then he added as we were nearly done with the walk, no near misses with cars or even stubbed toes having occurred, "And I am proud of you that you are being so independent, too." He is the only one I ever told about discovering all the textures beneath my feet that my cane had begun to show me. My parents did not need to know that, after all.

By the end of that summer, I had ventured well past my bus stop. My parents allowed me to walk anywhere within reason as long as I told them my plan. I had discovered new confidence in locating the curbs, steps, and streets I had never been allowed to cross alone before. I remember strolling six blocks due west and reaching our public square for the first time by myself, and thinking "It's my own independence day, too!"

I wish I could tell you the story ended there with happy walks into "normal." However, I remained throughout my schooling one of the only obviously disabled children that most of my peers and teachers had ever met. "We just didn't know how to deal with you," a former bully confessed to me thirty years later at a chance meeting. "It wasn't okay. You don't need to forgive any of it."

I remember at first being confused, then overwhelmed, by the nosiness, snubs, and bullying I faced. As a result, there was a period in elementary school when I longed to be old. Not only would this mean death would come sooner, relieving me from the growing daily stress of school life, but I saw how old people who were blind were treated with respect and gentleness. Why not me?

Within about a year, I hardened. Realizing I would never be accepted by most of my peers by the time I was in middle school, I adopted my own stances on social issues. I had nothing to lose, after all. Choked by the daily taunts and the overwhelming loneliness of simply being avoided in high school, I begged my parents and the school administrators to let me complete four years in three. Two summers of homework and staying inside were a very small price for sparing myself another year in public view. Why did I keep trying? I suppose something inside me still had faith, clinging to the hope of being somebody, somewhere.

Goaded on by linguistic accomplishment and curiosity, I became an exchange student to Switzerland when I graduated at age sixteen, unwittingly becoming one of the first official exchangees with a visible disability. Away from the town that still wordlessly considered me a community hazard, I learned that I could cast off the awkward images they held of me. But looking back, I still believe that that summer at age eight, and that walk toward independence created a pivotal moment, a trajectory into the "normal" world I still believed in, the "real world" I had always longed for, even when it did not long for me.

THIRTY-TWO

America

By Lauren Gatti

It is Friday night, 5 p.m. at the restaurant where I work on the weekends. We are in the garden area before the rush, wiping rainwater off patio furniture that no one likely will use. Sergio, Florenzio, Victor, Lorenzo, and I work efficiently and quietly, ringing out the rags on the bricks, taking in the May air and the apple blossoms that fill it from the tree next door. Minutes ago, before our manager stormed through and broke up the gaggle, we were standing inside discussing school. Most of the bus-boys—rather bus men, given that most of them have families and range in age between eighteen and forty—are taking ESL classes during the days, classes crammed between their two jobs in hotels and restaurants. Florenzio, the only one on the staff from Ecuador, not Mexico, is tired but happy because he just passed his level six (of eight) final on Wednesday. Victor, the oldest at forty, though, was quiet. He looked up and explained, "I burro (*I'm slow*)," tapping his temple with his pointer finger. "I no pass my test. Only level three." His voice is lilting and unsure, each syllable coming up at the end like a question, and then down softly. Florenzio encouraged him in Spanish: "Don't worry. You'll pass. You need to keep writing and speaking English more, though." Victor shrugged his thick shoulders and flashed that grin, sweet and hopeless.

Victor understands that voices are thin, frayed ribbons that he cannot hang onto forever. He has scraped together money to purchase a video phone, and every week he can see and talk to his wife, America Carmen, and his three children: Yolanda, who is nine; Manuel, who is six; and Brian Jose, who just turned five. I do not know how old America is, but I imagine she looks older than she is and that she tries to look pretty for the weekly date with her husband who aches for her a thousand miles away across a border. Maybe she braids her hair, or wears a purple shirt that compliments her dark skin.

After seven hours of work, Victor and I talk as we close down the restaurant together. He moves the big broom across the wooden floor professionally, having swept floors for a million years. I ask him about bringing his family over. "I do not know. Porque es dificil. Muy dificil. $12,000 for to bring here." As he fills the large olive oil container for me so that I can finish my side work, I can see that his eyes are tired. I look down. His sneakers are cheap and black, torn, splashed with bits of food from the frenzy of boxing up countless "to go's." He finishes his work quickly and efficiently, trying to catch the 12 a.m. bus so that he can get a few hours of sleep before his alarm wakes him up at 5:30 for his job at a downtown Chicago hotel.

Victor seems out of place among the sixteen- and seventeen-year-olds whom he works with, the young men whose wives are also raising small babies and children across the border in the pueblitos of Jalisco and Aguas Calientes. At our annual holiday parties, we all danced to the mariachis that our boss Larry hired and the bus staff paid to play over-time, and joked that we have the entire pueblos here at our restaurant. It is not far from the truth. Most of the men are related to each other. The entire kitchen staff is comprised of two families, cousins and uncles most-ly.

During the week I teach high-school English at a small school in the Pilsen/Little Village neighborhood of Chicago, where the majority of my students are from immigrant, Latino communities. Daniel is a student in my third-period American Literature course. Having come here only three years ago from Mexico, he was placed in ESL for his first two years, a small class of three or four given that almost all of our students are fully bilingual. Daniel is different from his classmates. He is clearly less Americanized than most of the kids in the school, and there is a humility that exudes from him, in part because of this. The incomprehensible gap between life there and life here is real and immediate to him; for others, less so, given that many of their parents came here for work when they were young. Their families are in Mexico, their *abuelitas* and *abuelos*, but most of them have not had to watch their parents scrape by in Mexico as Daniel has. They watch their parents work second shift at the factories here, instead.

Sometimes I imagine the towns in Mexico entirely inhabited by young wives and small babies whose deep black eyes have never seen their fathers or brothers. Towns inhabited entirely by *abuelitas*, who miss their children living in the bright and foreign country next to them. It is the voice they cling to, voices rattling across the dusty wires to the cement houses that glow pink in the sun. The voices, strange and comforting, of fathers and brothers and sons, grandchildren they have never held, utter-ing *feliz cumpleanos m'ija* and *cuidate* into ears hungering for hands and laps. But we all make due with what we have, I suppose. And these men have phones and two jobs and dark basement apartments shared with strangers from other pueblos in Mexico—strangers whose strange accents are even strange in a cold, white city called Chicago. The children, too, make due. With phones and mothers and dry Mexico heat, and promises. Promises are the corn, the meat. The promise of moving someday with a *coyote* across deserts that have no fences, or through rivers, dirty and wide.

Daniel is a small, thin boy with round glasses, and the shirts that he wears with his ties always look big and borrowed. He rarely matches, but always, inexplicably, has an air of neatness. *Buenos Dias, maestra*, he greets me cheerily every day. He knows that I am trying to improve my embarrassingly bad Spanish (I can barely make it into the past tense), and so he makes an effort to speak to me in it. He knows it makes me feel good.

Hola, Daniel. Como fue su fin de semana? Que hiciste?

Bueno. Trabaje.

Ganaste mucho dinero?

Si. Mas o menos. Veinte cinco dolares.

Twenty-five dollars, I think. Daniel has written about his job before. He works at a restaurant he spells "Mishigan Shores." He plates salads and desserts and sometimes waits on tables. I consider, guiltily, the $150 I earn from waitressing on the typical Friday night.

Daniel, whose father is dead, does have one sister by his real father. Yesenia is a freshman at school, and while I haven't met her yet, I secretly hope that I teach her when she is a junior. Daniel's job at the restaurant goes toward his and his sister's tuition at school—$400 a month, collectively. I think about this from the back of the room while Kate, my student teacher this quarter, gets the class focused. Vocabulary words are being reviewed, words floating through the back of my brain—*coruscate, ephemeral, pogrom*—birthing themselves into other shards of images: *Coruscating* rivers, *ephemeral* happiness. Factories. Videophones. Brooms. Deserts. *Pogrom*.

Teaching American Literature, I knew Melville had to appear, if not in white whales chased by a madman, then in the form of a difficult office worker refusing to do his work—refusing to do anything. So "Bartleby, the Scrivener: A Story of Wall-Street" it was. Bartleby works as a copyist in a lawyer's firm, and one day simply refuses to do anything at all, his mantra being, "I prefer not to." The lawyer/narrator of the story, although a self-identified lazy man, is initially flabbergasted by this refusal, but ultimately commits himself to attempting to understand Bartleby, who has no family to speak of, no home, no appetite, even. Bartleby ultimately dies after having been sent to prison as a vagrant. All of our students have internships in corporate offices, spending one school day a week there as a way to fund this Catholic education, so I was anxious to see what types of understanding they brought to a story like "Bartleby," a story that deals with offices much like the ones they work in.

The students are indignant after they read the story: "Why doesn't Bartleby just *do* something?" they ask. I am surprised by how frustrated they are with him. If Bartleby is unreal because he refuses to work, then the lawyer is ridiculous because he refuses to demand that Bartleby work. He baffles them. "If I was his boss I would just fire him. Why doesn't he just fire him? Jeez. They're both insane," one student spits. The class agrees. "What's wrong with this guy?"

Marisol is not vocal in class about how she feels, but when she hands in her paper, there is no question. It is entitled "Who's the Boss Now?" arguing that Bartleby exercises more power than his boss, who is more concerned with his "fraternal melancholy" with Bartleby rather than managing him at all. An employee who refuses to work means, well, that no work is done, no money made. The machine of industry stops. But the story of Bartleby and his lawyer boss could never be confused with the relationship the students' parents have with their own employers. Marisol wrote once of her father, an undocumented worker, whose boss subtracted the cost of the defective parts coming from his part of the factory line from her father's paycheck. And then there was the risk of additional penalties—most often a cut in hours. Her father's lack of documentation prevented him from voicing anything at all, and he was ultimately fired from the job. Marisol later, in a different class, wrote about witnessing his suicide attempt. Pills. Bathroom. Terror.

When asked to write about a time they had to do something they would have "preferred not to," like most high-school students, mine have no shortage of stories. But the students in front of me are different, in part because of the corporate internship jobs they work five times a month to cover their Catholic-school tuition. Most of them choose to write about these jobs. Alex writes: *I have been told to go clean up coffee spills from the floor or put signs in every men's washroom. I sometimes have to move thirty boxes from one floor to another. I along with others sometimes follow orders that are completely stupid . . . I only have the option to follow these orders so that I will not get a bad performance review or get fired. The only way I respond back is by working slowly and not get in any trouble . . . In order to work in a peaceful environment you have to sacrifice and in a way make compromises.*

Elizabeth has a darker tone. She discusses going to the mailroom, which she hates: *When I have to go down there I have to take the old elevators. They are ugly elevators. Then I always feel so uncomfortable because it's always packed with old guys. I didn't have many options back then and not today either. Only once there was a college intern and I had the option of asking her to go with me. I didn't though because I figured that even though I don't like going there I have to learn how to live with the bad things in life because they are always there.*

"Doesn't Bartleby have a family?" Daniel asked one day in class. The students puzzle through this, flipping through the pages of the story to sort it out. Jessica pipes up, "It says that the lawyer tried to ask about it but Bartleby didn't respond. So we don't know. But probably not." If Bartleby had a family, they must have thought, he would most certainly not refuse to work. This, of course, is beyond them. "I prefer not to" is not an option if one wants to survive. Victor or Daniel cannot say this, would not say this, because that would mean prioritizing their own idea of justice or comfort above what really matters: sending money to families in Mexico, or putting oneself through school, or paying a coyote to smuggle your family, scared and thirsty, over the border in the trunk of a car. Because it is not a matter of justice or pay or brooms or words—it is a matter of family, or survival, of videophones and working harder. It is a matter of America, sitting in the cool night. America, listening to street dogs bark and the radio's staticky songs and her children's voices sifting through open windows. America, preferring to imagine this as a temporary thing and that soon, very soon, Victor will be on his way home to her.

THIRTY-THREE

A Cultural Frankenstein

By Pao "Aegean" Yang

Part of me is *Hmong* man, part of me is US American, my origin is *Mong*olian, but
Scientifically, I am African. Part blues, part rock, part classical; part mentor, part
teacher, part poet and . . . I sold it, with origin and all.
Sewn together; refined by, fragmented by, culture and education.
Always changing, never static, I turn and twist to adjust my face:
Waking up too early and sleeping late,
Canceling and rescheduling with friends,
rushing and rushing to be up to date.
Only to be exhausted at the end; forgetting and losing my face.
I try to keep up with my many roles and many parts, much like actors do or a
person with a transplanted heart.
My right hand is a refugee camp in Thailand,
My left hand is the elders of my clan.
My heart is my home on a Saint Paul street, snow covered; the blood that flows is
in a dense forest on the high hills in Thailand, rain smothered.
And the entire me walks into the school where I teach
Where I try to build a safe space
for all parts of the mixed creature and race,
the vibrant being, my classroom community; my community is *this* beautiful
monster.
Perhaps the rest of the worlds do not understand; they are the ones usually with
pitchfork and fire in hand.
I do not use the bamboo switch my father used; it was a long-lasting and quick
burning pain. I use trust, hope, openness and vulnerability. In that there is no
shame.
While no riches come to me at the end of the week
and many bills sit on my desk in the kitchen

I get to live each day with eager voices, new questions, enlightening debates; The Power Of The Argument! Gathering reasonable evidence; these are critical thinkers, indeed.

I grow as they grow, their joy, their sudden inspiration, and their success
Are my payments, my gold, and my diamonds: my intrinsic rewards.

THIRTY-FOUR

Spirit First, Consequences Second

The Politics of Gender and Culture in the Playground

By Xamuel Bañales

HOME: NIGHT AND DAY

As a child, I loved the night—I still do. Staying up late was normal. Most nights I watched TV with my siblings or my mom, talking *chismes* with one of my sisters. The rattling of pots and pans in the kitchen was loud, and yelling and several arguments were common clamors that filled the house. After the last *novela* of the evening, most of the household retreated to sleep in rooms that were shared by many people. The noise, conflicts, and chatter disappeared slowly as the sky outside turned pitch black.

My mom, older sister, and I usually continued the night together in the living room. I listened to their intimate *pláticas* and stories, tuning in and out of their conversations. Sometimes there was silence or the humming of my mom's sewing machine. This downtime lasted about thirty minutes, other times the hours felt endless. The soft glow of the corner lamp created a sense of tranquility. Outside crickets chirped, and distant sounds of pigeons cooing or owls hooting travelled. Any anxieties we picked up during the day didn't matter anymore. Occasionally I dozed off before them; other times I was left alone to watch TV or stare at ebony shadows out the window. Charmed by the nocturnal energy, my pupils dilated like a cat's and my imagination ignited. I wondered about the distant stars and moon, the spider's silhouette that spun its web outdoors, or when my baby sister was due. Whatever the thought, it didn't

117

matter: I was happy that the magical night granted me a freedom I could not find during the day. The stillness connected me to my spirit, and I rejoiced.

I hated waking up early for school. I rarely did so without a painstaking struggle. There was no alarm clock, or anyone in particular to systematically wake me up. Since I slept on the living room couch in a crowded house, getting up in the morning was random. Every now and then I was awakened from the sound of the morning news that my dad watched on TV before leaving to mow the lawns, and trim the hedges and trees, of the millionaires living in the hills. Sometimes from the blast of blow dryers, creaking of faucets, or slamming of doors, as others bustled to get to work or school on time. Other times it was the grinding of car engines, or the smell of fried eggs cooking in the kitchen that interrupted my deep sleep. Once in a while, I heard a distant shout, "¡Ya levántate!" reminding me that I had to get up. Some days I slept through the entire morning commotion until my mom, who also had slept in, would shake me into consciousness, "¡Apúrate, mijo, ya es bien tarde!" Needless to say, showing up late during the first years of elementary school was common. In all the rush to leave the house, I was lucky if I had anything to eat. It was a good day if I arrived to school less than an hour late. Drowsy, with unkempt hair and wrinkled clothes, I nevertheless showed up to class.

RECESS AND THE FREEDOM OF HANDBALL

School was fuzzy, blurry. I didn't understand completely why I had to go and why so frequently. I also didn't know why my kindergarten and first-grade teachers didn't look like the students. These teachers were tall, white, had beards, and spoke Spanish with a funny accent. They were nice, though, and at times funny. My favorite part of the day was recess. As soon as the bell rang, students would jet out of the classroom like starving bats. It was as if our survival depended on every second of recess. I typically rushed to the basket at the corner of the classroom to get a red dodge ball before the others. Some days, under the blazing sun, I ran so uncontrollably to the playground it seemed like my feet barely touched the ground—as if I had invisible wings. In the seconds it took me to get to the playground, my heartbeat was like a hummingbird's flutter, and trickles of sweat cascaded down the side of my forehead. My smile, stretching from ear-to-ear, greeted the peach-colored handball walls of the black, paved courts.

If I was fortunate to have a dodge ball, I could be the first to play. Otherwise, I had to stand in line and wait for my turn. When this happened, sometimes I stood next to my classmate Lourdes as we waited. She had black wavy hair, was tall, thick, and tough. I liked playing with her since she was strong and good at hitting the ball firmly. We talked about things like our favorite colors or cartoons, but now and again we stood silently in awe, watching a good handball match.

Myrna, who was slender and had green eyes, was also good at playing handball. She was an expert at hitting the ball from far way or outside of the court, often in fancy ways too. I think one of my special talents was having stamina; I could play and play and never get tired. Few could match me. Often I played so much that the side of my hands would get grimy with *mugre*, and it took tons of soap to get rid of the grime. It didn't matter because I had fun as I lost myself in the physical and communal expression of the sport. Like clockwork, playing handball during recess and lunch became routine, and it was my highlight of going to school. Playing the game, I felt a similar freedom that I experienced at night.

One day, Juventino was next in line to play against me. Juventino—short, stocky, and sprinkled with freckles—had a jolly energy to him. He had a flat-top haircut, and we informally called him Juve in class. I was shocked to see him in line. This was the first time I ever noticed him at the handball courts. Pleasantly surprised, and with a grin of friendly rivalry, I welcomed him to a game. "You ready?" I asked. He nodded as I punched the red ball hard on the ground. The ball hit the wall and bounced to the far end of the court. Juve ran, almost missing it. Many of us giggled as we watched him struggle in the game. Although he looked strong, he didn't have much practice with the hand-ball-court coordination. He lost the round and went back in line with the others.

The next day, I asked Juve enthusiastically, "Are you gonna play handball again?" With a smirk on his face, he answered, "Yeah, I think so." I was happy to hear this. Perhaps we could be close friends? Maybe even be handball buddies! As the games continued, Juve's participation was comforting, but also simultaneously strange: his presence on the court made me aware that, besides me, he was the only other boy who played handball. For the first time, I wondered why this was so. Little by little, playing handball wasn't so much fun and normal like before. By the end of the week, Juve's initial interest in handball decreased. He played randomly and his appearances were inconsistent. In fact, he soon stopped coming to the court all together. From a distance, I would see him play kickball or baseball with other boys instead.

Juve's absence at the courts created a void, and I became aware that I was the only boy playing with the girls all the time. By rejecting handball, Juve had indirectly showed the school what he was not, in turn, revealing what I was: the only boy that played with Lourdes, Myrna, Verónica, Mayra, Ana, Maricela, María, Celia, Dolores, Mónica, Laura, Adriana, and many other girls. I questioned why I was the only boy that played handball and what was wrong with me. Other students wondered the same thing too: "He's a fag!" some gossiped as they passed me; "He's like a girl," snickered others; "Es un joto," I heard nearby. I didn't know what "fag" or "joto" meant, but I knew they were associated with being a girl, and that this was bad. I pretended not to hear them, but, like ghosts, their words hovered around and haunted me. The burden of this confusion, anxiety, and fear became heavy, torturous.

KICKBALL AND CONSEQUENCES

It was awful to be teased, to see evil sneers in the class. It was agonizing to hear laughs or whispers behind my back after school. It was mostly boys who did it, but there were unfriendly girls who also engaged in the tormenting. I didn't understand how I could be surrounded by so many people yet feel so alone. I bowed my head often, became hyper aware of my surroundings, and walked more cautiously. Eventually, it seemed like time and space collapsed, and my world fell apart. Playing handball came with negative consequences, and I had to choose to continue, or stop.

In search of solace, an idea came to me one day: What if I played kickball or baseball with the boys? Maybe the teasing would go away? Instead of playing handball during recess, I decided to go to the kickball field. This time, though, I didn't fly out of the classroom like I normally did. I sluggishly walked through the thick of the heat, taking my time to get to the field. Secretly, I hoped that recess would end before I got there. I tried to imagine what it would be like to play with the boys. I wondered what they would say to me. Would they even let me play with them?

With sweaty palms, I nervously approached the field. Carefully creeping up next to the boys, I got there as Moisés and Jorge were figuring out their teams, picking people to join. I was surprised to see Verónica immersed in the group. Nobody seemed to care that she was a girl, and she was even chosen to be in one of the teams without much hesitation. It was puzzling that she was the only girl playing with the boys and somehow not teased for this. Needing an even number, I was the last person chosen to join the second team. Stunned, I went along.

The game was not as bad as I thought it would be. I was pretty good at it, actually. I amazed many classmates when they saw how far I could kick the ball, and how fast I could run. We exchanged many laughs and smiles, and I returned to play again the next day. Some boys learned my name, and willingly picked me to be in their teams. I gradually became more comfortable with the game, but playing with the boys felt strange. It was weird to play in teams with people that had teased me at one point or another; playing with them felt fake at times. Plus, the boys didn't really talk about anything fun. They teased each other and said dumb things. I mostly stayed quiet.

One day after school, I walked home with Esmeralda as usual. She was friendly, wore a pair of gold earrings, and always had her long brown hair in a braid. We lived near one another and walking the half mile home together was fun. We talked about things like the shape of clouds, we picked out our favorites houses, and skipped along the sidewalk. We had a special connection. As we left the school grounds that day, my cheerful energy was suddenly smashed: "He's a fag," I heard again, piercing my ear drums like a burning needle. Jorge and his buddies pointed and laughed. Almost paralyzed, my heart felt like an anvil as my stomach hit the ground. I tried not to choke on the rock inside my throat, and went on with my way. Walking home, I didn't look up at the sky or admire any colors. I didn't talk to Esmeralda much. I mostly stared at the grey concrete ground as I walked in silence, numb. How could Jorge and his friends play kickball with me one minute, then tease me the next?

SPIRIT FIRST, CONSEQUENCES SECOND

The next day, on my way to the kickball field during recess, I paused as I walked by the handball courts. I questioned why I was returning to the place where Jorge, and other mean boys like him, played. It didn't make sense to be with people that liked me conditionally, temporarily, or not at all. Part of me wanted to go back to prove to everyone at the school that I certainly was not a fag or a *joto*, hoping I could erase their rejection and hate if I kicked the ball farther or ran faster.

As I looked behind my shoulders at the handball courts, like lightening, a flash of insight rushed though me. It wasn't playing handball with the girls that had consequences—not following my gender role is what created problems. It wasn't enough to only play with the boys. I had to be with the boys and be a "boy" all the time. The gender role and norms came first, the sport (and who one could be friends with, and what one could do) second. Gender determined which sport one could play—not the other way around. There and then, with passion and conviction, I was reminded that I played handball first. With awareness sharper than a blade, choosing kickball over handball would mean a spiritual betrayal— and this was worse than suffering the consequences of not conforming to my gendered expectations. I turned and ran to the handball courts.

I played handball that day like never before. Handball became more than playing a sport, it turned into an art form. Hitting the ball was like an invisible brushstroke that decorated the air. Everything felt different, clear like glass. The purple ice plants that decorated the playground appeared brighter, fuller.

It was mid-day but my pupils were dilated like a panther's at midnight. I had transformed madness into the beauty of a *mariposa*. The butterfly within had unleashed someone who challenges norms, the mundane, and contradictions, the one that renders complacency suspect, who reminds the world that it lacks flavor by revealing more color, the one that responds to the claim, "He's a fag" with an accentuated sway of the hips and a fearless stare—the one that found power in femininity. Being connected with my spirit was more important than following gender norms, and there was no turning back from my inner sense of sovereignty and justice.

That day, I learned that my physical expression in handball was really about divine truth and freedom. It was not the night itself, or playing handball necessarily, that granted me independence, but these things allowed me to feel alive. Although defying gender roles is not an easy process, I discovered the indelible lesson of revolution in all of this: that connecting with, and trusting my spirit is the root of my autonomy and existence.

THIRTY-FIVE

Forced Out at School

The Tenth Grade

By Erica Lenti

The school board continues to fund crappy lessons about Internet safety and the effects of drugs; but I am a teenager, and I think we know everything about everything and fail to listen.

In my spare time I play online games like Habbo Hotel and spend hours in lesbian lounges, chatting up girls. But on Facebook, I keep a low profile; I try to stay invisible.

My wallflower act pays off when I stumble upon a video by a friend of a friend. It's called "DYKE." Curious, I press play.
They're making fun of me.

I scroll down and read the comments, a dialogue driven solely on the entertainment of mocking me.

You know who the dyke is. It's E-R-I-C-A. Erica loves the ladies. Dykerica!
I am just a dyke.

I throw up my dinner, and then return to the computer to save all the comments. I throw up again and delete them from my hard drive a few hours later.

But I can't delete them from my head.

The way they laughed so playfully, the way they spit out my name on camera like it was their job, stays with me. For the first time in my life, I sincerely want to die.

I go to class the next day and take notes and try my best to stay invisible.

THIRTY-SIX

Torn

By Jia Curry-Bild

Jia Curry-Bild, student

Suzanne Linder, teacher

Note: This is a two-part description of an experience that a high schools student, Jia Curry-Bild, had with a teacher, Suzanne Linder. The editors had tried to include the painting Jia speaks of but were unable to get a good enough copy for the book. The experience itself is enlightening and we decided to include this piece without the visual art.

Jia:

Torn is a painting of two parts that reflect my experience as a transgendered student in high school. Identifying as androgynous (a lack of belonging to either gender, male or female), I have felt myself trapped between two different identities emotionally and without the ability to be open in my school, let alone the greater public. In the process of creating a painting, I employed two very different methods of working; in ink I tried a much looser free-formed method of moving media around, even mixing colors right on the paper. This was a representation of my mental fluidity—my ability to swap between genders and express one or the other. The graphite portrait was meticulously planned and laid out carefully, representing my caution moving out in the world and my fear of making a mistake or letting something slip inadvertently that could out me. Conversely, the expressions on each person's face show an expression that correlates to the other's representation—that is, the ink face is pained and worried instead of being free and fluid, while the graphite

125

person seems liberated and more at peace instead of restricted and closed off. Being an LGBTQ high school student is not simple, and in my work I tried to capture some of the struggle that thousands of other kids might be facing in their own lives.

Suzanne:

Jia produced the work she describes in the above paragraph as a final assignment in my Gender Studies elective. I've taught Jia for the last three years in required English classes and in the Gender Studies elective.

When Jia was a student in my sophomore English class, I assigned an essay in which students had to use their research to take a position on the question: Is there a gender gap in educational achievement and does it favor girls or boys? Jia objected to the binary nature of the assignment, and wrestled with what position to take and how to write the essay with integrity, when the presentation of the question was problematic. Over the course of the month while we did research, Jia spoke to me passionately and respectfully about their* objections to the assignment and what they wanted to write about instead. In the end, Jia wrote an essay about the bullying that LGBTQ students experience in high school and the impact that bullying has on their academic achievement. Jia's argument ended up being that the negative impact of the bullying of LGBTQ students is a more significant social problem than gender bias in the classroom. Throughout the experience (and in the subsequent two years) I was impressed with Jia's honesty, integrity, and vulnerability with me and with Jia's refusal to take the path of least resistance and do the assignment as written, which would have been far simpler and less risky than challenging me. Additionally, I learned an important lesson from Jia about the ways in which assignments that I might think of as benign can be marginalizing to students who don't conform to the gender binary.

As Jia's sophomore English essay topic suggests, they have experienced a not insignificant amount of bullying about their identity. While it has been painful for Jia, I have never seen them compromise their fundamental sense of who they are as a human in order to avoid notice. Instead, I have seen them grow stronger in their ability to articulate who they are and why they deserve to be treated with respect. I am humbled by the young adult that Jia is becoming.

Throughout this description, I'm using Jia's preferred personal pronoun "they/ them/their" in order to capture their androgynous experience of gender. As their last sentence suggests, "Being an LGBTQ student in high school is not sim-

ple . . . ," and Jia and I have discussed (and made various decisions) about what pronouns I should use when writing about them in relation to this piece and in the letters of recommendation that I wrote for Jia this fall.

Section Questions: Claiming Our Space and Identities

1. In this section, writers take power, describe power, claim who they are, who their students are. In what ways to they do this, whether African American in a white school, or blind in a sighted community, or in ways of language and culture?
2. In the first piece, "White Hallways," Cora-Lee Conway ends up "bursting through" and takes her spotlight. Have you had times when you have had to do this, when you have been surrounded by whiteness, or wealth, or because of homophobia or other situations? What could those around you have done?
3. The final piece in this section is visual art. The story about the art is a story of claiming how Jia Curry-Bild finds their own way to express what they experience, a story of claiming their own narrative. What other ways can you—or if you are a teacher, your students—express their strength, their resistance? Painting, sculpture, music, theater, dance?

Part VI

Celebrating the Power of Teachers

I like a teacher who gives you something to take home to think about besides homework.
—Lily Tomlin

Let's not play these kids cheap; let's find out what they have. What do they have that is a strength? What do they have that you can approach and build a bridge upon? Education is all a matter of building bridges, it seems to me. Environment is bouncing everything off everybody in this country. . . . The question is how can you relate the environment to yourself?
—Ralph Ellison, "What These Children Are Like" Lecture, 1963

I don't know what intelligence is. But this I do know, both from life and from literature: whenever you reduce human life to two plus two equals four, the human element within the human animal says, "I don't give a damn." You can work on that basis, but the kids cannot. If you can show me how I can cling to that which is real to me, while teaching me a way into the larger society, then I will not only drop my defenses and my hostility, but I will sing your praises and help you to make the desert bear fruit."
—Ralph Ellison, "What These Children Are Like" Lecture, 1963

The teacher is of course an artist, but being an artist does not mean that he or she can make the profile, can shape the students. What the educator does in teaching is to make it possible for the students to become themselves.
—Paulo Freire, *We Make the Road by Walking: Conversations on Education and Social Change*

THIRTY-SEVEN

Testimony

By Tasha Gaff

I imagined you waiting,
broken-wristed and black-eyed,
as I hovered by the doorway,
willing my expression neutral.

When I finally entered
I wanted to sit near you,
to rest my hands on your shoulders
and say, "Finished with your essay?"

But this is not my classroom,
and I cannot see your eyes
as the judge looks to me to tell
the whole truth without sentiment.

Your mother left you homeless.
You set the school on fire.

THIRTY-EIGHT

Seat Them with Princes

By Jeanne Bryner

It's winter in Brier County, and the biscuits that kept my hands warm all the way to school are in my belly. Jess sneezes just as Miss Lemley's finger points, and summons me to her desk during the arithmetic test. I figure it's all over for Jess and me. Miss Lemley has wavy, black hair that shines, and creamy brown skin. Today she's wearing a pink cotton blouse. If she didn't wear glasses, I figure she could be next year's queen of the Jack Town Fair. She even smells pretty. She don't smell like onions or bacon grease. Jess thinks she smells like honeysuckle, but I say she smells like a baby after her bath: all lotion and powdered. Dewyla Johnson claims Miss Lemley has white folks on her granddaddy's side, and that's why she's the color of chestnuts.

All the way to her desk I'm wondering if she watched us shooting at the crows before the bell rang. Our front pockets hold a fistful of lucky stones, and our slingshots are stuffed in our back pockets. Maybe she's fixing to give me what for 'cause I ain't finished memorizing my poem for the Thanksgiving play and those Ben Franklin sayings. Anyway, her hazel eyes are straight on me behind her glasses, and I just put my pencil down and mosey on up to her studying on how I will ask her if today's a good day to stay late and wipe down all the blackboards, pound chalk dust from the erasers.

"I have a note for your Mama, Virgil. It's very important. She needs to sign it and you need to bring it back tomorrow. Can you remember that?" I nod my head and forget to ask her about the blackboards and staying late. "Please remember, the note needs to be signed and returned tomorrow."

There's a mess of numbers waiting for me to add and subtract when I sit down, but it's the note burning a hole in my pocket like a quarter that takes the spit from my mouth, and makes it a crick in my hands. I figure after Mama reads this she'll pass it to Daddy, and then I will get the whipping of my life. Tarnation, why don't Miss Lemley just take me to the coat room and pull down the paddle? Jess and me only nipped one crow. I think that old bird could still fly. It wasn't killed. It wasn't even bleeding. Least we never seen no blood. I am thinking about reading this here note myself, but it is long hand and I only read print. If I show it to Jess's big brother, he'll get it dirty with his huge hands. Since the Kirby Mine slowed down, he helps his Daddy timber on Fish Pond Ridge, and the sap stays icky on his palms.

Every step of the slushy lane I feel my socks getting soggy and cold as my heart. I know I'm done for. At recess, I told Jess about Miss Lemley's note, then we buried our slingshots under a mess of leaves and one big rock down by Turk's barn. Jess says a teacher's note coming home, needing signing and all, well, it must mean trouble. It must be worse than getting all *F's*.

My Mama is busy cutting supper biscuits with a coffee cup when I drag myself through the door like a skunk-sprayed dog. She gives me the last oatmeal cookie on the plate and wants me to hurry out to feed. Side meat is frying on the stove, and I'm hogging that cookie down, half crying when I hand Mama Miss Lemley's note. "What's this, Virgil?"

"Jess and me we didn't hurt the crows. Maybe one is all, but we throwed the slingshots clear away, I promise Mama."

"Hush boy." First, Mama is reading and then, she's a wiping tears. She rubs her hands red as radishes under the spigot and dries them on her apron. There weren't a bit of flour or lard left under a single fingernail. She fetches her writing paper from the drawer of our pie safe cupboard, sits at the table with her ink pen and writes her name four times on a grocery poke. Long hand. Swirly. *Lavina Pearl Dawson*. She folds the note, all careful like a hanky, tucks it into a white envelope and seals it.

"Tomorrow, you take this back to Miss Lemley and don't you ever sass her, not ever. If you ever sass your teachers, Virgil, I'll be on you like poison vines choking a rail fence. Do you hear me?"

"Yes ma'am." She gives me a hug that nearly makes my oatmeal cookie come back up, and turns around, humming *How Great Thou Art* to her biscuits.

The next day I hand Miss Lemley back her note. I do not walk home with Jess that night. Miss Lemley drives me to town in her blue Buick. She has suckers in the glove compartment, and I get to pick any color. The red ones taste like cherries. All the way to town Miss Lemley's saying how good I'm doing with my reading and numbers. She says she is so proud of me. I don't want to bite my sucker. I can feel the rim of it pushing up against my mouth. I want to suck and suck this sweet cherry taste against my tongue and just hold it forever in my mouth. I don't want Miss Lemley to quit talking about me doing good with double words like *uphill* and *bobsled* and *tadpole*. She parks in from of Lester's Shoe Store and turns off her car. It has snowed six more inches and I can see my breath when we get out of the car. I stuff my bare hands deep into my coat pockets.

Lester opens his door. He's wearing his brown pants that whistle when he walks. "Howdy Miss Lemley. What's doin'?"

"Fine, just fine. We need to measure Virgil's feet."

"Yes ma'am." Lester turns and walks in front of all the empty chairs. The chain on his pocket watch makes the letter *U* and bumps against his soft belly.

Lester sits on a metal stool and waits for me to take off my shoes. I have to stand still while Lester measures my left foot and then, my right. Behind his ear, Lester has a mole the size of a tick. My sucker is all gone now, but I'm chewing the paper stick and studying the wild black hairs in Lester's eyebrows while he pulls a shoehorn from his hip pocket.

These brown shoes have a picture of a boy hugging his dog. The boy's dog is small, not a coon dog like our Shiloh. The shoes are stiff and shine like a new penny. The laces make a fine bow. These are Sunday shoes. I don't want to walk on the sidewalk for fear of stepping on spit-out-gum under the snow. I don't want dust or slush to ever hit these shoes. I don't want snow to melt around the soles and make water spots. In these shoes, I feel taller than our coal tipple.

Sleepy snowflakes are everywhere when we mosey out of Lester's. I run my hands along Miss Lemley's car and squeeze the snow in my hands. The snow is heavy. It's good packing snow, the kind Mama scoops into her big crock to make ice cream. Miss Lemley asks me if it's all right to throw my old shoes inside her car trunk. She will burn the shoes at her house, but only if I say that's all right. I tell her those shoes will make fine kindling. This trip to town, this stop at Lester's, the new shoes and boots, they are a secret she says. Not a bad sort of secret because Mama knows, but something we need never tell, not even to Jess.

THIRTY-NINE

Finding the Strength in the Fragile

By Kristy Pierce

She was sitting in the corner folded up like an infant, afraid to enter the world, hair covering her face, as if that would protect her from being seen. I remember walking over to her and telling her she needed to get up. In my role as a behavior/cultural specialist, parent, and adult in the school we both attended, I expected to have her comply. Instead she shook her head, no, still hiding under her dishwasher blonde hair. My initial response was shock. How dare she tell ME no. Who does this li'l girl think she is? I tried several more times to get her to follow my directive. She looked up and our eyes met. I no longer saw a defiant, frail, little white girl. What I saw was a look in her eyes that I don't remember seeing before. It was a look of sheer terror. Something in me knew she wasn't afraid of me, but rather afraid of the world and the people in it.

I chose not to engage with her and not feed into her fear. I let her know that if she needed anything I was here, but that she could not be defiant and do what she wanted to do. I think this is when we connected on some strange level. She knew I wasn't one to play with, but she also knew that for some unknown reason I understood her fear. I walked by a few more times to see other adults in the building, sitting next to her, talking in what I heard to be a condescending and enabling tone. Their voices were high pitched yet somehow comforting? Hearing them definitely brought up the "I hate when white people talk to kids in ways that embrace their weaknesses." I only know how to look fear dead its ugly face and keep it movin'. After all that's what I've had to do all my life. Wait Pierce! Not everyone has had to face their fears. Some people choose to live in that fear and let it hold them captive.

How could this little white girl be so afraid of a world that was supposed to embrace her whiteness, that was supposed to make it possible for her to have everything in the world she could dream of having? How could this not be her truth? Well, the year would go on and she would continue to hide in corners, not go to class, and be fearful of everything that crossed her path. I didn't spend much time with her except the occasional, "you have to get up off the floor and go to a room that resembles a classroom." She continued to defy me. So as with so many other children I work with, I kept it movin'. Yet, there was always something about this girl that stayed with me. Maybe it was her fear, maybe she was the little white girl who lived inside of me: the one who knew that I was supposed to be accepted and loved, but felt the exact opposite for different reasons. I was afraid of the world because although the color of my skin said I was black, my experiences were that of a girl who was white. I was born to a white mother from South Dakota and a black father from Jackson, Mississippi. As it turned out, I would not understand the real connection to this fear filled white girl until a year later.

The summer came and went. September 2013 and the school year started. Shame on me, but I didn't even think about her. There were new children, new families, and new challenges facing us. How could I possibly be thinking about my students from last year? First day of school, there, she was, like clock work in her "safe place." Nine hundred students, old and new, black, white, Latino, Hmong, Karin, Somali and every other culture under the rainbow were excited to see old and meet new friends. They had the same anxieties, fears, and excitement that I imagine she would have only hers were still debilitating and still holding her captive. I picked up where I left off with her. I guess I should give her a name now and call her Tina.

In her corner, by the door, there she stood. Her head bowed down, hair covering her face. "Hey Tina! Glad to see you're back. I'll walk you to where you're supposed to be." Then the all-too-familiar head shake letting me know that although things change, they also very much stay the same. I felt myself getting in my "black mama" frame of mind. I talked *at* her and told her that if she didn't come with me I would call home and she could try it again tomorrow, cause "I'm not doing this with you already this year." Li'l miss lady apparently has a lot more courage, will, and determination than some of my Latina and black girls. She dug her heels in like she was wearing concrete shoes. Clearly I was going to have to make her a believer in Ms. Pierce's word.

"I'm going to count backwards from five and when I get to one you betta' be taking a step, or as they say, tomorrow's another day." I started counting slowly and adding the .5s, eighth, and sixteenth, as I got closer to one to give her a little more time. I got to one and dang it if she didn't take a step toward me.

"Thank you, now let's go up to my office." Inside I was smiling, but on the outside? I let her know that I was way annoyed that she had taken up my time for what she would learn to understand my meaning of "foolishness."

Sometimes victories are short lived. It was like she was magic. We turned the corner to go down another hallway where there were students (people) and her courage instantly turned to terror. When I turned around to talk to her she had vanished. I know I'm getting seasoned, but even I know that people don't disappear, so where the heck did she go? I retraced our steps and found her around a little cove in the hallway,

"Girl, will you come on? I don't have all day to fool around with you." Now some would think I was being hard and not sympathetic, but really I was showing her strength. I would not feed her fear. The tone in my voice was letting her know that I wasn't going to let anything happen to her, but that I also wasn't going to let her do what she was so used to doing . . . sitting withdrawn from the life of the school around her. There were many days ahead of us much like this day. I'd get her from her "safe spot" but would have to talk her into simply moving.

On a daily basis various staff would see Tina in her corner. On a daily basis they would try to convince her to go to class. Some would bend down, or even sit down next to her and try to have a conversation with her in hopes of easing her anxiety.

The mornings would start with, "Ms. Pierce, would you help Tina get to class?"

Or I would see her and say, "Hey Tina, let's get going. I'll go to class with you." There went that head shake again. "Girl! What are you so afraid of?"

She talked with her head down and said something I could not understand. "I can't hear you. You're going to have to talk louder. I'm getting old and am too old to bend down, so you're going to have to speak up. If I have to bend over too long you're going to have to call the people to help me stand up."

I got a smile. Either she thought that was funny, or she imagined her small, frail, white girl self having to find the strength to straighten up this thick, black, and somewhat crazy woman.

She did stand up and said, "There are too many people, and they look at me."

What did she say that for, cause immediately I said, "Uh, excuse me, but there's people all over the world, and they only look at you like you're crazy when you're sitting in the corner. They won't even think about you if you just walk into the room and sit your li'l self down."

She did agree to walk toward her class. Then it was like her antilock brake system kicked in and those concrete shoes magically appeared on her feet again. "Girl! What the heck?" "No! There are too many people." Remember, victories can be small, but at least we had another one.

"Okay, let's go to my room, and we'll figure out how you can be in a school, in a class, with no people." She didn't quite catch my attempt at humor. I think she actually thought I would try to make that happen. I'm good, but I'm not that good. She stayed with me for the rest of that day and for several days after that and that's how we would bond . . . this thick, black woman and that frail, white girl.

I guess it was mid-October and the daily, "Ms. Pierce could you help get Tina to class?" calls on the radio had stopped. She was now waiting for me knowing that I wouldn't let her down and she *couldn't* let me down. She would be ready in her "safe place" with her three-ring binder and game face on. She didn't know it was her game face, her mask, but I did, and she knew I sensed how important it was to her. There was no more having to coax her, but more me stepping to her with energy of expectation, courage, and strength. If she didn't have her own courage (which she would later prove to have) she would have some of mine. We'd start by walking down the endless hallway to her class. I remember asking her what she liked to do. Shoulder shrugs and her standard answer, "I don't know." "What do you mean you don't know? Do you like to read, watch TV, play sports, or talk on the phone?"

"I would like to learn to speak Japanese and live in Japan."

Super shocked, "Well how's that going to work for you to live in Japan and you don't like to be around people? Girl! Don't you know there's like eight thousand people per square foot in Japan?" This was the first time I had seen her laugh. She hadn't thought about that part of wanting something, but it would prove to be something I would use every time she used the "too many people" line that she had come accustomed to using.

Together we were finally able to figure out how to get her to go into her first period class. Her teacher was amazing and did everything she could to accommodate Tina's anxiety, while holding her to the minimum standard of appearing in her classroom. She was given a special seat away from other students, in the back of the room, and where she couldn't be seen. It was still a daily challenge getting her into class, but with consistency, patience, reassurance, and persistence she made it. Her teacher knew that Tina had the will and ability to do the work, but needed to develop the skills to become a successful academic student. Weeks went by and first period was, for the most part, a success for both Tina and me. She got to class consistently with my help. I think she really liked the fact that I was her personal shield. I was her mammy, the one person at school who understood her.

One day during "our waiting to get it together timeframe," I was working on my computer, and she was sitting at her new "safe place."

I heard her more confident voice, one I felt blessed to hear, "I think I figured it out."

Me still working and not looking at her, "figured what out?"

"How I can go to class. If I have at least one friend in there I think I can do it."

Me still not looking at her, "That's great, but you don't seem to have any friends. How can you have friends when you're never in class?"

"Well I do have some friends, I just don't talk to them because I don't see them. I don't have them in any classes except one girl. Her name's Juanita (not her real name). I have her in one class, but I don't get to sit by her."

I credit myself as being a problem solver, so I began to make some phone calls to see if it was possible to change her schedule and her seating arrangements in that particular class.

"Wait! Ms. Pierce, I have some other friends in other classes too."

I asked her to name them then looked them up on the computer. Turns out one of her friends was a black girl, one was Mexican (this was her "best friend") and in another class there was a white girl she named as her friend. Okay, thoughts started swirling around in my head. How has Tina been in this school for going on two years and no one knows she had friends? More importantly what was it about me, a black woman, who could connect with her? Why did she trust me? Why did I like her so much? Questions, questions, and more questions. My goal now was to find some answers.

I sent emails asking if would be okay for me to let Tina start going to classes with her best friend. My goal was to get her to experience what being a student was like. As it turned out, it was the Mexican girl who would prove to be Tina's strength, not me, the adult. To date Tina attends every class with her best friend and is working on meeting new friends with the hope that her success will become less dependent on others.

As our relationship grew, so, too did our understanding of one another. I began to think about the historical significance of what I term the "mammy syndrome" means. The "mammy syndrome" is the role in which black women play as the nurturing, disciplinarian, and loving nonbiological figure in children's lives. For some this title is equivalent to a "nanny," however, for me the relationship Tina and I have developed traces back to slavery. It is much deeper than a paid position. It echoes back to the important and respected role that black women had in raising "massa's children."

Tina's story is a testimony to the art of mindful inquiry, or more simply put, to adults taking the time to look beyond the surface of what we see in our children in the hopes that maybe we'll see what's really there. Realizing that although we may have the experience, the degrees, and years of "expertise," the children are really the teachers. As adults I suggest we need to soak up all they tell us, absorb all our children have to offer. Imagine an educational system where we all become facilitators of learning and where we all learn from each other; across generations, across history.

FORTY

Piling On

One Teacher's Journey Toward Social Justice

By Lisa Cech

Directions in hand, I weaved up Highway 9, the Santa Cruz fog just lifting enough to see the tips of the redwoods. I blasted "Lovely Day" on my tape deck and sang along. Just two weeks earlier, I lived in Eureka, Illinois. I'd never seen an ocean or a redwood tree. Having spent my entire life in the Midwest, I'd also never seen a place where people like me could actually hold hands with our same-sex partners in public. The whole city of Santa Cruz, it seemed, was liberal—unheard of, and, for me, a relief!

By the time I left my resume-building job at Eureka College, alma mater of Ronald Reagan, I could barely recognize myself. Who was that woman working in the counseling department? I mean, I dated a *guy*, a nice guy, but a *guy*. I wore dresses (okay, only *one* dress, and it was denim) and my best friend at the college was a born-again Christian who frequently spoke of the "sin of homosexuality" after commenting, in the locker room, on my beautiful breasts. We worked out together. She ran for the Lord. I ran for my sanity.

I had some friends who had moved from the Midwest to Santa Cruz before I did. They'd told me about the place. From what they said, Santa Cruz offered more than oceans and redwoods. It promised a return the person I missed most: me. So one evening, I packed my brand new, bright red Subaru Justy, and fled. I left my grandma's cedar chest in the hands of my roommate. I had to make tough decisions, life-raft kinds of decisions, and that chest handed down through generations by Ulrike

Matilda Johnston just didn't fit. As a college basketball player, I was listed at six-foot-one in the program. I'm closer to five foot ten but still, I squeezed into that three-cylinder car surrounded by boxes, stereo speakers, my gym bag, and basketballs. I would have driven a sardine can out of Eureka. That's how desperately I needed to leave.

In Santa Cruz, I'd wanted a job in my field—teaching—so when the teacher's aide position for $6.05 an hour came through, I jumped at it. Now, here I was: wide-eyed, twenty-two, Midwest-born, winding my way through giant redwoods, ocean fog blending with the steam from the dark-roast *latte* I'd recently learned to love. All this, *plus* I was gainfully employed by the Santa Cruz county court and community schools program. Yeah, it was definitely a lovely day.

I checked my directions and turned in to the address on my scribbled note, excited to see my new school. I squinted through my windshield. Was this right? A gravel lot alongside a sagging volleyball net? Beyond the net, at the base of the Santa Cruz Mountains, sat a deserted church and a weather-beaten trailer. A set of not-quite-attached metal stairs led to the door that was tacked with a cock-eyed wooden sign: "Highlands School." Yes, I'd arrived. Early.

I waited.

Forty-five minutes later, a beat up Chevy Malibu pulled in, surf board sticking out the back, "Santa Cruz native" sticker on the bumper. A white-haired guy, slightly beyond middle age, lumbered out of the car. He looked rumpled, like he'd hit the snooze button too many times. His face was deeply grooved, and he had the look and feel of a guy that was over it. Over what? Well, everything. For the first time in my life, I felt overdressed in my khakis, blue blouse, and the slight heal on my Aerosol shoes. I hopped out of the car and introduced myself.

Jay waved off my outstretched hand, not in an unfriendly way. It was more of a "let's forgo the formalities and get to work" dismissal.

"Ever been a teacher's aide?" he asked.

"Well, no. But I have my teaching and counseling credential in Illinois, I just need to pass the PLACE to get credentialed here." I oozed enthusiasm.

"Unh," he said. "Where ya from?"

"Originally? Illinois."

He tossed his hands up and looked at the redwoods around us. "Keep this paradise away from your fellow Illinoisans, will ya?"

Throughout the course of our conversation I learned he was the head teacher at Highlands School, had been teaching thirty-five years, and he was clean and sober. By the time we reached the other side of the parking lot, I learned I'd be in charge of P.E., lunch, attendance, and suspensions. My orientation was complete, and Jay was gone.

Ten minutes later, students started arriving—not in yellow busses, but in vans from various group homes. Boys, no girls, emerged from the vehicles. They were the essence of in-control cool. They ranged in age between twelve and sixteen, and all had tattoos.

I'd been told I would be working with "at risk" youth. I wondered why "at risk" meant African American, Native American, Asian American, and Latino boys. I had never taught, not really, (I'd been a student-teacher for a few months) but I definitely had not taught for a school in which I was the minority in every way. I felt my stomach cinch. Honestly, I felt like I was the one "at risk."

I had taken a multicultural education class in downstate Illinois in which all but one of my all female classmates was white. As a college athlete, I had also played basketball with African Americans on my team. But as I stood there sipping my latte, I realized I had never been in a truly culturally diverse setting. I was by turns eager to get in there and try out my teaching chops, and just as eager to run headlong back down that canyon and look for a job as a barista.

When I stepped into the classroom, I was appalled. Where was the visual stimulation? How about those inspirational images, "Hang in there," with the cat dangling by one claw from a hammock, or "Reach for the heights," with the person summiting a mountain? The desks were a motley crew of mismatched orange, red, blue plastic in no particular order, as if someone had rolled them like dice and that's where they'd landed. Sections of the ceiling bulged out of their metal grids. The classroom coolly stated, *We don't care about you,* a message these kids were obviously used to.

Jay was at ease with the class. Somehow, in his rumpled way, he commanded student respect. I took attendance, and watched him closely, hoping to learn from a veteran. A few minutes later, Jay tossed me the volleyball and motioned to the door. I caught the ball (hoping the guys would notice my athletic prowess) and looked back expectantly toward Jay. He stayed in the classroom.

I was excited to get outside and half-trotted to the sagging volleyball court. While I tried to tighten up the net to "regulation" height, the guys straggled to the court. I told them I'd officiate, and I selected a team to serve first. I'd played competitive volleyball in the past, so I figured I knew a few things. Two plays into P.E., I called a double-hit on Mike Martinez, because it was a blatant double hit, the overhand kind that I could not let slide.

"Fuck you, bitch," said Mike, six-foot-three, thick-necked, well-muscled, and strong enough to kick the ball and send it whizzing so close to my head that I had to duck, after which I watched the ball sail over the parking lot and off school grounds.

Now P.E. was over.

The boys scattered, some pulling out cigarettes, others heading to the street. I scurried around trying to get them back inside the trailer. Panicked, I ran to get Jay, but he was not in the classroom. Fifteen minutes later, I found him sleeping in his car.

That was my first lovely day.

After work, I went to my friends Georgine and Ellen's house, and I cried. "They hate me." I said. "I can't believe I spent six years studying for this job, and I suck at it," I added. G and E, as I called them, had been together ten years when I met them. They were a model gay couple, weathering the storms of intimacy and being *out* when *out* was not *in*. "They don't hate you. You're so cool, Lisa," they encouraged.

"No seriously, I suck at this, *and* they hate me," I shot back.

"Look it's your first day, it's bound to get better, now sit down and eat some baked ziti," Georgine said. Georgine, a New York Italian, made some outrageous ziti.

The carbs made everything better for the moment. G and E asked me about Kelly, my first love interest since I'd moved to Santa Cruz. "We got us all tickets for the Kate Clinton concert. You better call Kelly and let her know." That gave me something to look forward to. I couldn't wait for the weekend.

I went back to work the next day. Mike Martinez had been suspended, and at first I felt good about it. My one day without him there was comparatively easy.

Before school started on the day Mike returned, his group-home van pulled up next to me in the lot. His "case managers/parents" told me he had "anger issues," and they were working with him on expressing his anger in an appropriate manner. Since I also had counselor training, I understood this. Excited to share my book-learned expertise I said, "Have him try some deep breathing, and for a lot of people, counting to ten works too."

"Yeah, mostly we let him punch the hell out of the heavy bag," they said.

The group-home parents pulled away. I felt reassured to learn that Mike's case workers agreed with the suspension, but something nagged at me, like when the tag on your shirt brushes your skin, and you scratch at it to make it go away. But five minutes later, it's there again. I just didn't feel right. I tried to catch Mike, to talk things out a bit, but he had already made his way to the classroom. I survived that day and headed home.

After only three days of teaching, I was feeling signs of burnout: a painful cold sore erupted on my lower lip, and I was too exhausted for my daily workouts. This did not bode well for my teaching career. But the weekend reenergized me. After we all went to the Kate Clinton concert and laughed our asses off, Kelly and I went to my place to catch the 49ers game. True to my Midwestern roots, I'm a Bears fan, but I went with it just so Kelly and I could hold hands. *Damn*, I thought, *This must be serious.*

The 49ers, favored to win the Super Bowl that year, looked great. Joe Montana and Jerry Rice. For a sports fan, what's not to love? Mostly, Kelly and I talked, but we actually watched some of the game, and there was one play that stood out, to me. Roger Craig, their running back, got stacked up at the line of scrimmage. But then a linebacker slammed into him, then another, and another. They just kept piling on. Finally, the refs threw a flag. Even though I was not a 49ers fan yet, I yelled at the TV, "Hey, he's down! Enough already!"

Kelly looked at me. "I guess you're kind of intense about sports?" she said.

"Uh, yeah, I guess so," I answered. But I felt that scratchy tag again—like maybe it wasn't just a missed football call that got to me that day.

Later that evening, I walked Kelly out to her motorcycle. We kissed. We held each other. In that moment the failure I felt at work melted away.

The next morning, running a little late, I jogged to my red Justy, still feeling that kissing high. I angled around to the driver's side ready to jump in. Then I saw it. In dark black letters, someone had spray-painted "DYKE" on my car. It covered the entire door.

I'm not sure how long I stood there, trying to register it. My heart pounded—fear, shame, panic—all these things pumped through my veins, then my capillaries, eventually reaching my cells. That's how it felt, like the shame was cellular. I spent some time blaming myself. Maybe I shouldn't have kissed Kelly out in the open, I thought. Maybe I deserved this. I stood there, tears brimming.

Then I just got pissed. "I'm in fucking Santa Cruz, are you fucking kidding me?" I screamed it; I kicked my little Justy's wheel. "This isn't Eureka, Illinois mother fuckers." I paced. I wanted to hit things.

My thoughts felt like a pinball bouncing from bumper to bumper. Who did this? Was it that surfer across the street? Shit. Should I call Georgine? Should I go to the car wash? Who the fuck would do this? Why? I pictured driving to work with the word "dyke" painted on my door. *Fuck*!

I sprinted to the house, cleared the four front stairs in one leap, and ran to the kitchen. I grabbed a sponge and some 409. Breathing hard, back at Justy, desperately, I scrubbed, but DYKE would not come off. I had no choice. It was my second week. I *needed* this job. So, with DYKE on my door, I drove. To work.

I arrived late, in the middle of first period. Jay gave me the eye. I shrugged my shoulders. Mike sat in the back of the room. I smiled at him, and he scowled back. Shit, I thought, *I'm trying here*. I looked at the clock, and hell if it wasn't P.E. time again. My heart pounded. I took the volley-ball and looked at Jay. He pointed with his chin to the door.

My first-day enthusiasm considerably dampened, I walked slowly to the net and stopped. I thought of the morning. I thought of the spray paint, and of Mike calling me a bitch. I felt the anger rise in me again. Across the net, Mike stood with fists clinched, daring me to say or do something. It was a bit like looking in the mirror, his face pinched, eyes squinting at me: my face pinched, thinking about this morning. I tossed the volleyball from hand to hand, took a deep breath. I guess Mike and I *both* have "anger issues," I thought.

But on a deeper level, I thought, What if we're both pissed for good reasons? What if *pissed off* is the only healthy response to this specific kind of bullshit?

"Dyke" on my car happened once. But it felt like the hundredth time, to me. It was an accumulation slights, of hatred, of seeing signs: "Gays must die," of people telling me who I AM is wrong. It felt like all these slights were piling on me.

And I began to think maybe that Mike felt crushed, too. And then, I came along. I didn't even know him or ask to understand *his* way of playing volleyball. I just told him the way he had always played volleyball was *wrong*. Next, a thought dropped into my head. What if my double-hit call felt like things piling on Mike? What if it was like that extra linebacker in the 49er game after the whistle had blown? I wasn't the only lineman on his opposing team. There were cops and judges and teachers and administrators and shop owners all representing systems who had ignored, condescended to, and maligned his culture, rules, and ways of being who he was. *Bam, bam, bam* — and if you're going to do that too, Lisa Cech (system, judge, teacher), then, "Fuck you, bitch."

At least in the 49ers game, the refs *finally* threw a flag. But no one had thrown the flag for Mike. Or for me, for that matter. So maybe I wasn't a ref, but I knew that in this moment, I could do more than yell at the TV. I could make a choice to say, *It's not okay. Enough already.*

There, on the ragged volleyball court, I took a deep breath. I looked at my Justy parked with the word, Dyke, facing away from us. I looked at Mike Martinez. "Mike, you start us off. Show us how it's done," I said. I handed him the ball.

Mike took it from my hands, walked to one side of the net and served. I stuck my whistle in my pocket. Jay peeked out from the classroom, and I wondered if he'd actually been watching last week, too, because he gave me a thumbs-up sign before he closed the door.

Mike and I coexisted at Highlands School for the next few weeks. I wish I could say we became close, like in those inspirational teaching movies. But the truth is, Mike still barely spoke to me. Weeks later, my teaching credential came through, and I got transferred to another school. Jay caught me after school on my last day. "So I guess you're going to be a teacher now?" he said.

"Yeah, I think they're going to put me in Watsonville."

"Well, good luck, it's not easy, but don't let it get to you." He squinted into the sun. "Here, this might help." He handed me a thick, dog-eared book. I assumed it was a meditation book, or maybe a find-a-new-career book. I tossed into the back of my car.

That weekend, I hung at the Saturn café as I did most weekends, trying to learn how to teach again. I knew I'd be responsible for social studies, math, and P.E., so I had my work cut out for me. I brought Jay's book with me as an afterthought. A history major in college, I'd never heard of *The People's History* by Howard Zinn. After my third cup of dark roast, I opened it and started reading—and I could not put it down. It provided a cultural context I'd never had before. Somehow, in his rumpled-veteran way, Jay knew what I needed.

Years later I exchanged the ocean and redwoods for the 14ers of Colorado. I got a job in Boulder as a TOSA: teacher on special assignment, supported by a federal grant. The grant title—Safe and Drug Free Schools—was synonymous with my job description. I was to keep our district "safe and drug free." I worked in every school in the district on creating a positive school climate. Annually, I administered the High School Youth Risk Behavior Survey. The results served as a wake up call to the community: 40 percent of our students were bullied, 30 percent were binge drinking, 15 percent had considered suicide.

But when I disaggregated the data, the full story became more clear: 60 percent of our students of color were bullied; 40 percent of our students of color were binge drinking, and 25 percent or our students of color had considered suicide. It was like watching two busloads of kids pull up to our public schools: one bus was dominated by kids of color. These were the "at risk" youth. It looked a lot like the bus that had pulled up to that court and community school long ago. I thought of Mike Martinez and felt that volleyball whizzing by my head again.

I've heard arguments that suggest something is inherently wrong with kids of color, something that makes them less likely to "achieve" (the gap, again) and more likely to take risks. But those theories have been disproven over and again.

Way back in Santa Cruz, Mike and Jay started me on a journey to try to understand what I experienced in there. Zinn's book gave me the historical context I'd never learned. After that, I read every book I could about equity, diversity, and social justice. I took classes and went to conferences on how the "isms" impact our students and our institutions, including schools. I got involved in district equity work and eventually became an equity trainer. The more I read and participated in what I have come to call "The Work," the more the overall landscape came clear.

But I couldn't do much about my new learning, since I held an administrator's position. I was no longer there, in the trenches, *in the classroom*. It bugged me. What bugged me even more was, now I was teaching *teachers*, but I had not worked directly with students in a long time. So, I made the choice to go back to teaching and counseling, to work directly with students.

It scared me. It excited me.

I sought out the most diverse building in my district. I landed a hybrid position: part teacher, part counselor. The opportunities to apply the framework I'd spent two decades studying and teaching came flooding into my office and classroom. And this time, no one said *Fuck you, bitch*, at least, not to my face.

Still, one particular situation put my years of study to the test. Maria and Estrella almost got into a fistfight in the hall one day. "Sassy" did not even begin to describe Maria. The girl had 'tude. She was a finger-wagging, hips-cocked eleven-year-old. She talked to me often, and though I was not supposed to have favorites, Maria was mine.

The conflict between the girls involved generations of family trauma and drama. It all started when the girls were in first grade. The energy they spent on their mutual hatred had always affected their grades. Now they were at risk of suspension.

"Before you do that," I said to my principal, "Let's try mediation." I didn't want to lose Maria.

I called both Maria and Estrella down to my office *at the same time*. There was so much vitriol between the two girls that when Maria saw Estrella sitting in my chair, she refused to enter my office. When she finally did enter, the tension was thick. No one talked. Not Maria. Not Estrella. So I broke the ice. I said, "Why are you two so mad?"

"I just don't like her, Miss," said Estrella.

"Yeah, we hate each other, okay?" said Maria.

"But *why*?" I asked. They rolled their eyes. I tried other, more counselor-like questions, but nothing dented them. Desperate, I said, "Okay, how about you agree to just leave each other alone?"

"We can try, but it's always going to happen," said Maria.

The numbers on my digital clock never flipped so slowly. When the passing bell rang and we were still sitting there, I gave up. I decided to take a risk that scared me even more than I'd been scared that first day I taught in Santa Cruz.

"Okay, well some day, when you're older, I'd like to talk to you about what I think is *really* going on."

They perked up a bit. "When we're older? Why not now? Tell us, Miss," Maria said. "Tell us now," they said, together.

"No. You'll think I'm weird," I said, a little too much like an insecure middle-schooler. But that familiarity must have snagged them.

"Just tell us, Miss, maybe it will help."

Maria's almost-willingness surprised me. So I took a deep breath and said through my own fear, "Do you know what discrimination is?"

Their voices overlapped. "Miss, we're Mexican. We kinda know what discrimination is." They spared me the implied "duh."

I pressed on. "So tell me, how does it feel?"

"It feels crappy," said Maria. "They call me beaner. They make fun of my accent."

"They tell me my skin is always dirty," Estrella said. "They think we're stupid because our parents don't speak English." At the mention of parents, they looked at each other.

"I thought your dad was in ICE," Maria said.

"He is. He's legal now, but he's still there. He got in the car with a guy who got a DUI."

At the age of twelve, these girls knew the acronyms DUI and ICE. Put *those* terms on a middle-class IQ test, and see how the kids fare then.

"Have you ever talked to someone about it?" I asked.

"No," they said, again in unison.

"Is it possible that all this anger you feel at being discriminated against makes you so mad that you don't know what to do with it? So instead of getting mad at the people who tear you down, you tear each other down?" I waited. Then I added, "You fight for reasons that don't really matter. Like how Maria wears her hair, or how Estrella walks. Because it's easier than recognizing that you're angry at something else. Maybe angry at the people calling you a beaner?"

Another silence filled the room. But it was not like the one we began with. In this silence, both girls hung their heads. When they finally looked up, tears streamed down their cheeks. It's not professional, I know, but I felt tears warming my face, too. We—the three of us—sat in the room, saying nothing. I passed the Kleenex around.

"So, do you think I'm weird?" I tried to break the tension a bit.

Both girls shook their heads, no, tears still welling. We cried some more.

"Sometimes I take it out on my sister," Estrella said.

"I take it out on my mom," said Maria.

"Yeah, we take it out on our dogs, our little sisters, because we don't know what we do with it," I said. "We don't talk about it, and it just builds up." I waited, then I added, "I'd like to hear your stories sometime, if you want to tell them. I know I'm white, but . . ." At that, the "duh" was no longer implied. The girls rolled their eyes at me and I laughed a little, wiped the tears from my cheeks. "But I'm trying to be a white person who makes it better, not worse, so, well, just know that you can talk to me."

From there, the two girls began to talk, for real. They caught up on the lost years, compared stories, and even started to giggle, like middle-school girls.

"Okay, I'm late for my class," I said. "I'll write you both a pass."

"Miss, can we stay in your office and talk?" Maria looked at me, pleading.

I halted a minute, not out of fear, but to hold this moment a little while longer. "Sure." I said. I closed the door, knowing that two days ago I would have never left these two alone in an enclosed space.

Somehow that nagging I'd felt for years finally went away. It felt good to acknowledge the different treatment that accompanies "difference." So many of us were taught to be "colorblind." We thought it was the right thing to do. "I don't see color, I only see students," was our mantra in college.

But when I looked at Maria and Estrella, at Mike, and hell, even at myself—I realized, our differences makes us who we are. My difference makes me, me. To say we don't see it is a lie. And all students sense bullshit a mile away.

When I came back to my office after class, Maria and Estrella asked if they could stay in my office one more period.

"Now, you're just working it." I said. "Back to class."

They laughed, but didn't put up a fight. Maria stood by my desk. "I'm going to social studies, and Estrella is going to math," she said. I signed their passes and handed them to each girl. "Thanks, Miss," they said in unison, and then they looked at each other, and giggled.

Section Questions: Celebrating the Power of Teachers

1. In each of these pieces in this section, a teacher figures out who she or he is, how each can connect to his or her students. The teachers come from many different backgrounds and experience. What do you think makes it possible for each of them to make that connection? What do they have in common?

2. In "Finding the Strength in the Fragile," Kristy Pierce learns, over months, about her student who is afraid to go to class. She takes her time. In what ways does she show patience? What does she realize, at the end of this piece, about her connection as a black woman, to her white student?

3. Lisa Cech, in "Piling On," learns in different contexts about her students. She does this by learning who they are as individuals, not as representatives. How does she grow on the job? What conclusions does she reach about race and its connection to education, success, and failure?

Part VII

Reaching Across Difference and Celebrating Diversity's Richness

The educator has the duty of not being neutral.
—Paulo Freire, *We Make the Road by Walking: Conversations on Education and Social Change*

"Controversial" as we all know, is often a euphemism for "interesting and intelligent."
—Kevin Smith

Dominator culture has tried to keep us all afraid, to make us choose safety instead of risk, sameness instead of diversity. Moving through that fear, finding out what connects us, reveling in our differences; this is the process that brings us closer, that gives us a world of shared values, of meaningful community.
—bell hooks, *Teaching Community: A Pedagogy of Hope*

The differences were plain enough, and yet I saw that they were as nothing compared with what we had in common. As I lay in bed at night, the sky outside my window reflecting the city's dim glow, I thought about Abuelita's fierce loyalty to blood. But what really binds people as family? The way they shore themselves up with stories; the way siblings can feud bitterly but still come through for each other; how an untimely death, a child gone before a parent, shakes the very foundations; how the weaker ones, the ones with invisible wounds, are sheltered; how a constant din is medicine against loneliness; and how celebrating the same occasions year after year steels us to the changes they herald. And always food at the center of it all.
—Sonia Sotomayor, *My Beloved World*

FORTY-ONE

People-Colored Crayons

By Julie Feng

This is an ode to people-colored crayons
in a Kindergarten classroom, a bucket
of wax pastels wrapped in brittle paper.
Blunt branches of amber and russet
and pale sand and sable. The flicker
of red in cinnamons and golds in gingers,
the warm ochres and nutty sorrels,
the coppers, coffees, creams, and olives.

The five-year-olds survey the
tawnies and khakis and burnished browns,
hold sticks up to their palms,
compare hues to their fingers, consult
classmates on whether the right one
is more beige or sienna.

In the moment they find the precise flush
of skin, they combat every Band-Aid
on the wrong colored knee, every pair
of supposedly-invisible pantyhose
which render so many invisible, force
naked every nude fabric and sole.
This is an ode to the worth of colors and choices,
to acknowledgement, to consciousness,
to the very first self-portraits people draw.

FORTY-TWO

"Red Light, Green Light"

By DJ Savarese

Round and round and round
they roll, voices blurred
by the pulsating beat
and metallic whir
of wheels on wood.

My fellow kindergartners—
curly-haired Nikki
and half-grinning Julia,
Austin in his baseball cap,
and Lisa of the trampoline.
"Deeeej," they squeal,
a kind of moving sun, hands joined, reaching,
stretching, hoping to add me
to their ray.

They don't see autism yet,
don't know that I've been "included."
1 and 1 and 1 and 1 makes 4
and 1 makes 5. . . .
The disco ball freckles us
with light.

"Red light," the Skate Station manager
exclaims, and we drop hands,
careening like cars on an icy bridge,
arms and legs flailing.
Nikki bumps Julia

who yanks Lisa.

And Austin trips.

I staccato past,
unable to stop.

Later, bare-toed and sandaled,
I stand at the exit of the roller rink,
blinded by the sun.
"Green light," Austin whispers,
gently taking my hand.

FORTY-THREE

Walking Down the Corridor Is Being in Another Country

By Julie Landsman

Released from first hour,
students pour into the hallway.
Hands on hips, some shout:
You tol' her you thought I was with her man last night you know that's not true.
Others walk by in orange, blue or purple scarves and veils.
In stairwells young men pray and bow —
    cramp into a space to bend toward mecca.
White girls put on make up, spike up their hair with black polished fingernails,
    pull at rings in their noses and lips.

A hush of Hmong slips through gaining volume as girls giggle
after huddling quiet in the corner all during science lab.

Five minutes of hip hop, earphones curved over heads: the latest Outkast.
One young man takes dreaming steps, tuning into Monk's piano:
    a CD his father gave him in the hope it might calm his son during long
    afternoons.

Someone prays and someone sings and someone cries;
    one quiet, hungry girl who never knows where she is going
    slouches against a corner of the third floor hallway.

Noise thins,
    teachers pull doors closed in unison, calling to their students as they might
    call to their own children on an early evening in November when
    the light has changed and they want to begin dinner.

A boy speaks quickly, Liberian accent,
a girl from Eritrea slaps palms with her friend from the Northside,
Mexican music syncopates from the lunch room
    where study hall is just beginning.

Silence,

a flat surface of doors.

The young girl who was crying darts into the bathroom.

Women in uniforms patrol with walkie-talkies: crackle from the office
    "Fight in the parking lot"
    voice back,
    "I'm comin, honey, are the cops on their way?"

Hallways stilled: two lovers press up against the lockers on the second floor,
laugh deep into the skin of each other's neck,
keep a lookout. Between glances they touch and touch and touch.
Second bell, they arrange hair and clothes, buttons and lips, drift to class.

After they have gone, silence,
except for a whispered prayer in Somali
as a single delicate boy bends his body toward the eastern sun.

FORTY-FOUR

A Visit to the County Special Ed Program

By Mary Langer Thompson

They fly on top of balls,
swim on mats.
A woman tosses fabric over a child's head
and a girl flaps her arms atop a cushion.
The boy in a highchair has a face full of oatmeal.

One comes close to gaze at me.
"Hello," I say.
She keeps staring.
"She'd like to hold your hand.
Show you around," says an aide.

A boy talks of his cousin, Mario.
"He died," he says.
As if I need help, he puts hands palm to palm,
then onto one side of his face.
He tilts his head and repeats, "Died."
"I'm sorry," I say,
wondering who's observing whom.

FORTY-FIVE
Breaking the Ice

By Lisa Richter

Their names perch in various poses,
carefully rendered on folded rectangles
of lined paper on the table in front
of them: Lalitha. Afsaneh. Zuhaira.
Mohanna. Samira. My students tell me
their countries: Bangladesh, Sri Lanka,
Pakistan, Ethiopia, Iran. Some have
lived here for fifteen years, others, five
months, all living nearby in Regent Park
or St. James Town, concrete high-rises
whose names crackle with Englishness,
vestiges of a wistful aristocracy.

My not being married worries them.
Deep in my thirties, untethered
to children or husband, this life seems
aloof and untenable, strange-tasting,
a tea that's salted rather than sugared,
the herbs picked at impossible altitudes,
infusions unfamiliar to the tongue.
They are shocked to learn
I am not twenty-five, intrigued that
my hair and eyes are dark as theirs.

Where are you from? they want to know.
How can I tell them I myself do not
know for certain; how for centuries,
Russia and Poland and Romania housed

167

then expelled my family as bodies
reject foreign objects lodged within them,
how to explain *Ashkenazi* or even Jewish
as ethnicity, not religion.

I stick to Toronto, hear the surprise
and envy cluck in their mouths, clink in
gold bangles: my birth in this city,
my white-but-not-white-ness,
my ability to speak in the rapid
currents of English that sweep them
up from riverbanks, grasping for roots
or stones to hold onto.

It is winter, and we step onto new ice
together, our steps measured
and tentative, words chosen and delivered
with the careful deliberation of explorers,
until laughing, almost crazy with relief,
— — — — we reach the other side.

FORTY-SIX

Chasing Butterflies and Catching Grasshoppers

By Elizabeth E. Vaughn

In February 1960, a group of young people decided to eat at the Woolworth's lunch counter in Greensboro, North Carolina.

This became known as a "Sit In," a peaceful beginning of the civil rights movement.

In 1947, my hometown sign read, "Lynn Grove—Population 100." Lynn Grove, Harris Grove, and Brown's Grove were small, thriving rural communities, within a few miles of each other. Lynn Grove and Harris Grove were named for my ancestors, the Lynns and Harrises. Brown's Grove was named for someone else's ancestors. Lynn Grove had its own grocery store, general store, post office, feed mill, two service stations, three churches, a grade school, high school, and was surrounded by miles and miles of flat farm land.

Our family lived on a hundred-acre farm, with an old farmhouse, small tenant cabin, barn with concrete silo, apple orchard, small wooded area, and a red fox. There were also cows, pigs, and crops. Blanche and Odie lived in the tenant cabin. The cabin had one long front room, a small back room, and kitchen. There was no bathroom. Blanche helped Mamma in the house, and Odie helped Daddy on farm. I had no idea that they worked for my parents, that my parents supplied a place for them to live and paid them money for work. Our farmhouse burned to the ground while we were away from home. No one was hurt, but we had nothing left.

After the farmhouse burned, Blanche and Odie had to move away, because we had no place to live, except the cabin. The couple would come to visit with us from time to time. They both had very dark skin, and were always well dressed. Odie was big and handsome in a suit and tie, and Blanche once wore a yellow suit, yellow hat, and high heels. They both had big, pretty white teeth, big smiles, and laughed loudly. Blanche had very long legs. When Odie picked me up, my white arm could not reach around his huge dark neck. I knew that Blanche and Odie loved me.

In the spring, Daddy and a man named Albert began building a new house for us. Daddy and Albert had green eyes and the same last name. They worked laying concrete block, building concrete forms, sawing, and hammering. I would ride the saw horses, play in sawdust, and build things from lumber scraps. Every morning I would go running into Albert's arms, and he would pick me up, high in the air, saying, "Der's dat pink baby." I loved Albert and rode on his back while he laid heavy, gray, concrete block. Albert never complained or asked me to climb down. One morning I went running into Albert's arms, as was our routine. Albert smiled, picked me up into the air, I hugged him and he said, "Der's dat pink baby." That morning, I said to Albert, "Der's dat black baby." I could tell from the expression on my parents' faces that I had said something horribly wrong. I didn't intend to say anything wrong. I was simply told, "Don't say that again. It might hurt Albert's feelings." I didn't understand what I had done wrong, but I knew there was no way to repair it. I had hurt Albert's feelings. Albert never called me his pink baby again.

By the end of the summer Daddy and Albert had completed construction on the new house. It was brick veneer and bright white stucco. I had my own bedroom, painted blue, with a bedroom suite built from white pine. He also made me a swing, suspended between two cedar trees. He put a rubber hose on the chains that held the swing, so the chains would not hurt my hands. A few years later the road in front of our house was paved. Life was so near perfect that I did not want to go to Heaven, with streets paved of gold. I did not want to leave Lynn Grove. Lynn Grove was near the Tennessee border, with Kentucky Lake nearby. There were hills, tall evergreens, with dogwood and redbud trees blooming in the spring. The sun shone on the lake so brightly it hurt my eyes. There were picnic tables, picnics, a dip in the water, and fishing. An uncle or cousin would bring to my attention that there was a fish on my hook. I would pull it out of the water, and my picture would be taken with my catch. I was quite happy with the new blacktop in front of the house that made smooth riding on my bicycle. Who would want to ride on gold? That would be more blinding than the sun on the lake. I was happy with chasing butterflies and catching grasshoppers.

Float like a butterfly, sting like a bee.
  —Muhammad Ali

One of Daddy's sisters, who lived in Chicago, mailed me a tough, stiff, heavy stuffed bear for Christmas, the winter we lived in the cabin. The bear was bigger than I was and the perfect boxing opponent. My mother's nephew was a big, blue-eyed, well-built, handsome man, with an amazing smile. He was a Golden Gloves boxing champion and that meant he could whip anybody or anything. By age three I was a boxing fan. The words golden and champion were enough for me. My boxing champion cousin would watch me hit the bear and have me leave the bear on the floor to hit him, a real human being, as hard as I could. By that time I was old enough to attend school and play at recess, my favorite subject. I was always chosen by the boys' team. I fought to win.

I'm a fighter. I believe in the eye-for-an-eye business. I'm no cheek turner. I got no respect for a man who won't hit back. You kill my dog, you better hide your cat. —Muhammad Ali

Every day I came home with bruised legs and the sash dangling from my crisp starched and ruffled dress.

It's just a job. Grass grows, birds fly, waves pound the sand. I beat people up.
  —Muhammad Ali

As an adolescent, my love of the fight and boxing caused me to become a fan of Cassius Clay, the Louisville Lip. Clay said it himself, "I'm the Greatest!" My high-school chemistry teacher had once been Clay's sparring partner, prior to Clay winning the Olympic medal, so this almost made me personal friends with Ali.

My hometown, Lynn Grove, was tobacco fields, tobacco barns, apple and cherry orchards, grazing cattle, watermelon in the summer, with tulips, lilacs, daffodils, and all colors of irises in the spring; but all was not well. My mother awakened me early one morning, our old light blue Plymouth loaded with some possessions. My mother, sister, and I left the new house. I was eight years old, and this was totally unexpected. We left Lynn Grove, and I never lived there again. We were not homeless; we just weren't in our home. I was okay at first. It was summertime, and we stayed with my mother's brother and his family. I got to play on endless summer days with my cousins, but at nighttime, the house was crowded. We were going to have to move. We moved a few miles down the road, into my great aunt's home. There was more room, but there were no children running through her house, banging doors and making noise. At nighttime, I began to miss my Daddy and Lynn Grove.

My great aunt's house did not have a floor, furnace, or bathtub. It had a coal-burning fireplace that made the air smell like rotten eggs. There were ashes and cinders to remove every morning. It was cold, dark, and dismal: no sunshine, no diamonds in the grass, no flat land. There was just rough, ugly, strip-mined ground. It was stripped of everything green: no grass, no weeds, and sparse trees. The landscape was sand rock, the remains of coal outcroppings, and cane breaks where deadly rattlesnakes and copperheads lived. The stripper pits were filled with huge, long, nasty-looking water moccasins.

I would soon start a new school, away from Lynn Grove. My mother kept me at home the first day of school. She told me that she was afraid there was going to be trouble. I didn't know what this meant. My cousins were allowed to go to school. Why did I have to stay home? Wouldn't I get in trouble for not attending? I begged to go, even though it was a new and unfamiliar school, I had plenty of cousins who would be there. Mamma was right about the trouble. There was plenty of it. The town was filled with angry people, newspaper and magazine reporters with television cameras, state policemen, and a National Guard unit. One woman was attempting to take her child into my classroom. The mayor of the town and other powerful men had met and declared there would be no integrated school in their town. My teacher-to-be had been threatened. She, her son, and the one black child walked into the elementary school building, the walkway lined on both sides by state policemen and national guardsmen. She taught that first day of school with two students, her son and the one black child.

He who is not courageous enough to take risks will accomplish nothing in life.
   —Muhammad Ali

My mother had not kept me home because she disapproved of integration. She had kept me home because she anticipated violent, angry, dangerous mobs of people and possible rioting. She didn't want me to get hurt, and she probably did not want me to see what she feared might happen. She protected me from the display of angry people, who were fueled by powerful, wealthy people. People against the integration effort lifted the car belonging to the black woman, turned it around, and told her to go home. A few rural towns, with minimal black population, had been hand selected for integration. A.B. "Happy" Chandler was Governor of Kentucky, and, perhaps, wanted to be president of the United States. Poor communities with low population were targets that could be controlled. Men of wealth and small political importance could be easily manipulated; and they were often unaware of the manipulation. The wealthy men had a chance at power, and fame, by wielding their power within their own small communities.

The integration effort made headline news, but the politicians and their constituents weren't the only people being manipulated. The news portrayed them as angry and ignorant. It was generally believed the mother of the black child had been paid to enroll her child in the elementary school. Whether or not money was involved, she must have believed this was the right thing to do. She had the backing of the governor, powerful politicians, and men in uniforms with firearms. I don't know what the truth was, but the angry crowd must have frightened her away. The child did not return to school the next day.

There was unrest for weeks. I was finally allowed to go to school, still afraid I would be in trouble for playing "hooky." I had not been sick, and I had no idea what had gone on just a few miles from me. At the school, the state police were gone, but National Guard soldiers camped there for weeks. At recess children would talk to the guardsmen. I was among the girls in love with the handsome soldier from New Jersey, whose nickname was Daddy-O. I had just turned nine years old, and Daddy-O was at least eighteen or older. Girls from grades one through twelve had plans to marry him. We were heartbroken when the guard left.

The guards had not been there to entertain us. They had camped on our playground because one child, my age, had attended school, in my classroom, with my teacher, the one day I was kept at home! The attempt to integrate that school had failed. The angry crowd had made national news, and the national news had exaggerated the hostility and ignorance of the crowd. Some horrible things happened, but by the beginning of the next school year, almost all the commonwealth's schools had begun to integrate. This time, teenagers, not nine-year-old babies, were enrolling in the schools. There was minimal discussion about blacks now being in the white schools, but there was something that was going unrecognized in this fight for educational equality. The black students were about to lose their schools, their ball teams, and their teachers. While they were being assimilated into the white schools, the black teachers were going to lose their jobs, and there were going to be a lot of vacant school buildings. The schools made room for black students. Enrollment increased and classes were crowded, but there was no noticeable change in the number of teachers. In western Kentucky, we had integrated classrooms with students of different races, but the faculty was not integrated at all. Student sports would soon be dominated by black athletes, but the educators remained predominately white.

The Greensboro, North Carolina Woolworth's "Sit In" was still a few years away, and I didn't know anything about it when it occurred. Our local schools had been integrated throughout most of the commonwealth, without the dramatic incidents that preceded full integration. Integrating the schools eliminated all the good rival basketball teams, but the newly integrated schools now had great basketball players spread out on each of the teams.

Hating people because of their color is wrong. And it doesn't matter which color does the hating. It's just plain wrong. —Muhammad Ali

I knew about segregation in education, but in this case, by age. My birthday fell in late August, making me one of the younger students in my grade. Our church used a different "cut-off" date for placing students by age. I went to school with junior-high students, but had to attend Sunday school with the elementary-grade students. My mother even talked to the pastor, who held a doctor's degree in theology, asking that I be allowed to attend Sunday school with my classmates and sit with them in big church. The response was, "No." I was like Rosa Parks in the back of the bus. This was a rigid rule and there would be no integration by age.

This made no sense. My sister started college a month after she turned sixteen. I would become a teenager in Sunday school with students in junior high. The words from the pulpit were the same to the congregation, but from where I sat, the message was different. I did not belong in either group. I was not invited to the church school activities my schoolmates attended. I could listen to the same sermon, and be exposed to the same information, if I sat in my section. I could tithe, just like everybody else. I would sit in church, thinking I could imagine how a little black kid must feel, being the only black child in a room full of white people.

The school was integrated, but the movie theater was still segregated. Tickets were priced by age, not color, but whites sat on the main floor and blacks watched the same movie from the balcony. The problem was that white teenagers wanted to be in the balcony, and that was not allowed. The balcony became forbidden fruit, making it more enticing, more fun. Adults could not see what went on in the balcony. Popcorn could be thrown from the balcony with anonymity; there was no control over what was said aloud; teenagers could kiss and make out in the balcony; and it was the best place for watching Peter Pan fly. White boys and girls would sneak up into the balcony. Black boys and girls had no reason to sneak down to the main floor. They already had the best seats. We went to school together, sat by each other in classes and in the lunch room. It didn't seem so much segregation by color as it was age. Finally, the balcony was closed to everyone.

All of our education was not in the classroom where classes were held, but between the classes, before classes, and after classes. One of the most popular boys in high school was black. He was a football player and good student. More importantly, he knew how to open a pocketknife very quickly with a flick of his thumb. No switchblade was needed. All the boys wanted to be able to be as quick at opening a pocketknife as he was. Between classes and at lunch break, boys would stand in groups by the lockers, under his tutelage, trying to perfect this skill. There was never an intentional cut made by one person on another. No one was ever threatened, no one hurt by another person. The white boys were happy, bleeding and butchering themselves, trying to perfect a skill that one greatly admired black boy had. Our school was full of white boys with Band-Aids on their thumbs and fingers. Today it is a felony to possess such a weapon on school property. Under certain circumstances, a juvenile may be tried as an adult, facing one to five years in the penitentiary for merely possessing a knife at school. Exhibiting the knife-opening skills my classmates had learned would be unthinkable. If that had been the law in the sixties, there would be few high-school graduates, no college graduates, no doctors, no lawyers, no bankers, no merchants or any other person working, whose job might be denied because of a felony conviction. My high-school buddies would be felons, with the only job opportunity being to commit more crimes.

Friendship is the hardest thing in the world to explain. It's not something you learn in school. But if you haven't learned the meaning of friendship, you really haven't learned anything. —Muhammad Ali

The summer of 1964 fell between my junior and senior years in high school. My mother had married a lawyer with three small children. I called him Daddy D. During this same summer break, my sister was chosen to teach art in the Governor's Honors Program in Macon, Georgia. I was sixteen and had a driver's license. We began the journey from Western Kentucky, through Tennessee, to Georgia in her old dark green Ford for her summer teaching job. It was hot and humid, with no air conditioning and shimmering steam rising from the pavement.

I attended summer school in Macon in the mornings, gaining credit for Senior English. Macon maintained separate public high schools for boys and girls during the regular school year. However, the summer school classes were not segregated by gender. Boys and girls were allowed in the same classrooms. Teaching was intense and high quality.

Family members of the honors faculty didn't have to be honor students. Since my sister was an honors faculty member I could attend any class I wanted to attend. As soon as the high-school English class ended, I would drive to the college campus for an honors class. It was so hot I could not touch the steering wheel without wearing gloves. I sat on a terrycloth towel to avoid being burned. People were dying from heat stroke. The average high temperature was 105 degrees.

I was never homesick, but I was needed at home and had to leave Georgia. Mamma had been bedridden as a result of injuries received in two automobile accidents and needed help caring for the children. I had completed the summer-school program in Macon and wanted to stay with my sister, but a flight had already been booked for me. My mom also found Verna around this time, even before I returned. Verna's grandmother had been a slave. She was an imposing, tall, black woman.

Her posture was straight, and she wore a white uniform every day. She loved us, and did everything for us that my mother was physically unable to do, including some kind of discipline I still do not understand. She and my mother were best friends.

When I landed, Mamma, Daddy D, and Verna met me as I got off the plane. It was hot and humid, and we were hungry. The four of us went into The Green Gables, a large, nice restaurant. It was not the Woolworth's lunch counter. People were staring at us. We were seated at a table near the center of the restaurant. Verna was the only black person in the restaurant. One man, with his family and one black woman, had successfully conducted one small town's first "Sit In." It was a subtle, powerful, landmark event. We had simply eaten a meal in a restaurant.

In 1968, I applied to law school. Now I was back in sex-discrimination world, not race discrimination. My admission test scores were unimpressive, but Daddy D said, "All you do is pay your money, and you get in." I argued with him, "It isn't that way anymore." He insisted, "You pay the money, you get in." Some law schools did not want women (that is why Hillary Clinton went to Yale, not Harvard). I am convinced the school decided they would admit me on their own before they would be forced to do so.

I was unaware that the Equal Rights Amendment, which had been proposed by Alice Paul in 1923, was going to be introduced to Congress in a few years. Men and women were terrified of what this might mean. The "Separate, but Equal" theory of providing education applied to race, not gender. Although women had worked building ships and airplanes, had attended institutions of higher learning, and had become scientists, doctors, and lawyers, there was but a sprinkling of them working throughout the states. There was fear women might not stay home and be proper wives and mothers. There was a campaign to glorify the homemaker: vacuuming, mopping, having the whitest white laundry and the best meals for a family to "come home to." What if women began to take men's jobs? What if men had to do women's work?

Evelyn M. Lord was the only female faculty member in my law school. Evelyn had been elected to the Delaware State Senate and had five children. She had the respect and admiration of faculty and students. Before going to law school I had heard rumors that female law students were not well accepted by faculty, nor by students. But because of Evelyn M. Lord and the female librarian, our lives as female students were made much easier. We became somewhat accepted by the remainder of faculty and students. We integrated the law school. Each year there were more women applying to law school. More and more women were being admitted to the bar, practicing law, even appearing before judges and juries. Very slowly, the distinction between lawyer and "female lawyer" or "woman lawyer" began to dim. People who needed legal help didn't really care about the gender of the lawyer providing legal help. It remained a struggle with peers, judges, and everyone else involved in the legal system. Interestingly, the twenty-first century led to more women becoming lawyers than men.

The spring semester of my junior year in law school, there was a young, handsome, new instructor. He had worked as an assistant US Attorney. I had no classes with this instructor. He invited me to go fishing. We drove from Louisville to Frankfort, the Capitol, on a beautiful spring Friday afternoon; fishing gear in the back seat. He showed me the limestone outcroppings, high hills, deep valleys, the view from the high point in the cemetery, historic spots in Frankfort, and we waded in a picture book stream. This stream might have had fish in it, but I do not remember catching any fish. No fish appeared on my line, as they often did when I was a child, fishing at Kentucky Lake. I'm sure there was some kind of background music; maybe "Lazy Bones" or "What a Day for A Daydream." With no fish, we returned to Louisville for dinner. Dinner was at the instructor's apartment. I was beginning to think we should have gone "out" for dinner and was a little nervous. I'm not sure I was old enough to drink, but the handsome instructor opened a bottle of wine. I didn't have a lot of experience with alcohol. While I was in high school, my parents had made a deal with me: drink as much as you want, whenever you want at home, but you must promise to never drink on a date. We kept our deal. Law students couldn't afford to drink alcoholic beverages and much preferred marijuana. After the instructor had a glass or two of wine, he told me he had pulled my transcripts and looked at my grades. Then he started telling stories about his work at the US Attorney's office. He bragged that he was in the room when the draft board met, discussing Cassius Clay's draft status. Proving his inside information, boasting about his position, he told me that one of the draft board members had said, "I don't give a damn what he (Clay) says about being a conscientious objector, that nigger's going to the army!" This professor had researched me. He also knew the truth about Clay and what went on behind the scenes at the draft board. That evening was over. Somehow I made it home from our first and last date.

I wanted to tell everyone in the world what had happened to Mohammed Ali. He never had a chance to be declared a conscientious objector. I wanted Ali to know, but my knowledge would have been determined to be rank hearsay in a court of law. I had no idea how to make this information public. It is still hearsay. I cannot prove it.

In 1976, a newspaper reporter called my office and made an appointment to interview me. A friend of mine was in my office when the reporter arrived. The reporter was waiting for me in the reception area. "Hey," my friend said, "there's a really pretty man out in your lobby." Indeed, there was a tall, dark, and handsome man waiting to interview me. He was wearing a three-piece black corduroy suit, and interviewed me about an old building I was rehabilitating. He did publish an article some months later in the Sunday section of the newspaper. By then though, he was burned out on writing. We married in 1983.

I found out over the years that during my husband's career as a sportswriter/editor, he sat in the press box with Muhammad Ali and Howard Cosell. He knew I had a huge crush on Ali and would not discuss Ali, nor boxing. I began to wonder if it was true, if he had really met Ali. Then one day, we flew from Florida to Louisville, and were the first people off the plane. As we stepped onto the runway, a tall man called to my husband.

My husband responded "Hello, Howard."

"Who was that?" I asked.

"Howard Cosell," he replied, and kept walking. He really did know them, but he would tell me nothing of Ali.

Many of the great heavyweight boxing champions were black, except for Rocky Marciano. My husband didn't object to my having a George Foreman grill, a collection of books on boxing, or rattling on about Joe Louis. He brought me a Rocky Marciano souvenir T-shirt from a trip he made to Brockton, Massachusetts. I even had an older client, who had been a boxer and went by the name "Baby Joe." He was a short, strong, black man, with enormous hands. He won my husband's heart. My husband helped me take care of Joe and would even cook breakfast for him. Joe claimed to have worked out with Barrow, and been married to one of Barrow's sisters. He told a lot of stories, which sounded as if they might be true. He never spoke of the Brown Bomber as Joe Louis, just Joe or Joe Barrow.

In the summer of 2013, my husband and I were in Louisville with our identical twin grandsons. Grandchildren transform a lot of people and "The Boys" had transformed us. They had made us silly, goofy, and scared about the future, before they were ever born. We were very proud grandparents. "Look at his poop. This one just peed in my face. That one just smiled. Did you feed this one or that one? Which one is this? Here, hold this one. Take that one." Life had changed, it was hectic, and it was wonderful. "Did you see that? Did you hear that?" The first five years were more like living in an ongoing experiment than having a life experience. We were the people to avoid at school functions, social gatherings, and cocktail parties. We knew only one subject: "The Boys." Their grandfather has declared them "The Zenith."

On the way to Louisville to visit the Muhammad Ali Center, their grandfather, my husband, told stories about Ali. Who was this man and what had he done with my husband? Had he accepted my infatuation with another man? We spent hours at the center. It was the greatest: Leroy Neiman art, art by Ali, a place to hit a punching bag, a spot for shadow boxing, films of boxing matches, a relaxation area, and a section devoted to the early days of the civil rights movement, a drug store counter, and film footage of school-integration efforts.

That film of school integration struck a nerve. I watched the clips several times, studying carefully, listening carefully, and looking for anyone I might recognize. It took me back to the fourth grade, and that first day of school I had missed. I returned to this part of the exhibition, looking, wondering, and trying to remember. This was a snapshot of American school history. I had been part of it in a small way. No one knew that about me: schools, lunch counters, movie theaters, and separate drinking fountains. Our grandsons had no idea what I was talking about. They were as innocent as I was when I hurt Albert's feelings. Our home had been filled with children from different races and cultures and ethnicities from the time our daughter began kindergarten. Now she had these wonderful children. I didn't know where to begin to describe what life was like back then.

It would soon be time for "The Boys" to return to school, new clothes, new teachers; then Halloween parties, fall break, and Christmas. We went to a big family Christmas party, brothers, sisters, cousins, close cousins, distant cousins, and people no one recognized. Everyone was welcome and had plenty to eat. Gifts were exchanged, followed by an informal, family trivia contest. There were no prizes for correct or incorrect answers, except for laughter. "How many times had Kaye been married? (She didn't know the correct answer). Who made Ann's wedding dress? What song did Kaye sing at the Junior Opry in Nashville? Who made her dress she wore on stage? Why was Jim sent home in the first grade? What was the name of Dale's dog? Who called Daddy from jail?"

I knew who called and why he had called. My fine, upstanding, respected businessman cousin had a broad grin on his face. He didn't wait for the response. "I was wrongfully convicted," he laughed. "I was pushed out into the street." For the benefit of everyone under sixty, he explained about the integration effort at my grade school. He told of the hysteria and near riot frenzy. Someone in the crowd yelled out, "Hey jig-a-boo, why don't you go back to the jungle?" The Kentucky State Police asked the person who made that remark to step forward. No one admitted to saying it, but a boy pushed my cousin out of the crowd and into the street. He was immediately arrested for someone else's speech. He had his daddy to come get him from jail. Free speech was expensive.

The man who views the world at fifty the same as he did at twenty has wasted thirty years of his life. —Muhammad Ali

All these things, these trips, these struggles, made up one life, mine. Mine. And all this time I learned racism was not a genetic defect. It was learned behavior.

"Float like a butterfly, sting like a bee."

FORTY-SEVEN

Breaking Bread

By Merna Ann Hecht

I believe poetry, like bread is for everyone
. . . . in the unanimous blood of those who struggle,
—Roque Dalton

I don't know much about the bread
that Abdi, Farah and Hodan,
my students from Somalia, eat,

I don't know what ingredients are kneaded
into the dough of their survival,
I don't know if it's flatbread or risen.

Farah writes how once he put his ear
to a road in Mogadishu
and heard an aria,
how he can still see children
playing a jumping game
caught in a leaping moment
lifted from blood-stained streets.

Hodan says her blood is lost
because it still belongs to the flag
of her Somali star.

Abdi tells me his mother
has sworn him to secrecy,
how his father has already used
an entire month's earnings
to surprise him

with what will be his first
suit, for graduation,
Abdi, whose heart
is like a beautiful fruit,
tender and exposed,
who tells me he believes
this is an America that will allow him
to become a lawyer for truth
and justice, even a judge.

Children of goat's milk, red dust,
stringy chicken, scarcity
of grain and water,
I know the Somali wind
that once sang your lullabies
is a cutthroat wanderer
who drifts in each night
with his blood smell of tribal battle.

Thinking of Somalia, brown hands over open fires,
bread shared in a circle of wizened eyes,
hungers beyond my imagining,
my thoughts leap to a restaurant table
in Seattle, though it could be San Francisco,
Sun Valley, Aspen, New York, with a waiter
who says "My name is Josh
and I'll be your server tonight,"
where the privileged dip
focaccia or ciabatta
in exclusive oil
cold pressed and extra virgin
and read the novellas
that menus have become,
to assure themselves the eggs are local,
the cheese artisan, the ostrich organic.

What if the next fad pulls
its self-important palette
away from the local and organic
and features food from war zones
packaged for the hungers
of the well fed.
Goat meat from Somalia,
pounded grain from Sudan,
Iraqi dates covered with bitter
chocolate,
it could happen,
it could happen that the bread of struggle
will be sold

as the empathy of eating.

I want to tell Farah, Hodan and Abdi
that I know about chickens,
how they lay eggs warm in the hand,
with yolks that are simply determined
truths of yellow,
that I am not impressed
with the notion of slow food
because many of us already know
whatever is at high speed is dangerous,
and we don't need Josh
to tell us what the old Somali or Iraqi farmers'
hands have been doing for centuries,
that I wish Abdi could become a judge
and that good bread and its unanimous communion
would be what we learn to break together.

Section Questions: Reaching Across Difference and Celebrating Diversity's Richness

1. In all these poems and in the prose piece, there is hope and a firm belief in the children and young people who enter our school doors. Find evidence of this hope and belief in each of these poems and the prose selection.
2. Elizabeth E. Vaughn, in her essay "Chasing Butterflies and Catching Grasshoppers," brings us the perspective of history. She captures a time of intense segregation in her Southern upbringing and the progress in her life. She intersperses Muhammad Ali's career and quotes throughout. How can we make this history alive for those in our classes? Can we find ways to integrate oral history projects into our schools, all our schools, to capture the multiple lenses through which we see our world?
3. What will it take for our schools to be come places of celebration?

Part VIII

Subversive Teaching and Learning

Because subjects like literature and art history have no obvious material pay-off, they tend to attract those who look askance at capitalist
notions of utility. The idea of doing something purely for the delight of
it has always rattled the grey-bearded guardians of the state. Sheer
pointlessness has always been a deeply subversive affair.
—Terry Eagleton

In the end, we will remember not the words of our enemies, but the
silence of our friends.
—Martin Luther King Jr.

Any startling piece of work has a subversive element in it, a delicious
element often. Subversion is only disagreeable when it manifests in
political or social activity.
—Leonard Cohen

FORTY-EIGHT

How I Learned to Read the Word

By Francisco Rios

I grew up in the mostly Latino/Chicano west side of Denver, Colorado in the 1960s and 70s. The local, public high school that I attended was nearly over 80 percent Latino/Chicano, though we had only a few Latino/Chicano teachers in the school. It was a particularly challenging time given public unrest and protests about the Vietnam War as well as calls for equality from a variety of social identity groups as part of the broader civil rights movement. Our community was central in the Chicano movement that was occurring, primarily throughout the southwestern United States. Our school, myself included, participated in the school walkouts, called "blowouts," that were occurring in Chicano communities across the United States. It was in these moments that I was strengthening an emerging critical consciousness about oppression, resistance, and the power of student activism.

In eleventh grade, one of the few Latino teachers pulled me aside and encouraged me to consider going to college. It was the first time the very idea of college was planted in my mind. With the idea that I could go to college swirling in my head, I was fortunate to be accepted into Upward Bound—a federally funded, college-preparation program—in between my junior and senior year. As I moved into the senior year, I decided to take one of the very few, and my first, college-preparatory class that was being offered at my school: College Prep English.

***

As I walked into class that first day, I was immediately struck by the fact that the student demographic of the class was nearly all White despite the overall make-up of the school. Only two other Chicano students and I were in the class. I did not even know some of these White students in the class attended our school despite the fact that we were almost all seniors.

The other notable characteristic of the class was the teacher: Mr. Allen. Mr. Allen was young, only a few years out of university, with a short haircut and small wire-rim glasses. The business suit he wore hung on his thin-built frame. He had classical music playing in the background and was sipping tea with his left pinky sticking out when I first saw him in class.

As he began the class, he talked about the books we would read and mentioned that we would go as a class to the Denver Art Museum. In my mind, I was hearing this desire to assure we were "cultured"—as if the vibrant cultural community around us was not "cultural" enough.

The first book we were assigned was *The Picture of Dorian Gray* by Oscar Wilde. I began to read the story of Dorian, a wealthy young man interested in preserving his mortality so he could engage in his own sinful living in pursuit of his own self-gratification. It was, quite honestly, completely foreign to my life experiences.

I distinctly recall, as I was walking home from school one day, thinking about my own life in juxtaposition to that of Dorian. I walked home along a particular path to assure that I would be safe, away from the gangs that were starting to form in our community. I recalled looking at some of the houses and the obvious poverty of some of the people who lived there. I almost stepped on a used prophylactic that was on the sidewalk. I thought if this is what life has in store for us, why would anyone want to live any longer!?

I could not "connect" my own social condition to that of Dorian Gray. I chose, at that point, to engage in what Herbert Kohl calls "willful not learning." I did not read the chapters assigned for homework the next day nor did I answer the questions that were to be posed to the class for homework.

As I returned to class that next day, Mr. Allen walked down the aisles asking students to share their answers to the questions from the homework assignment. He stopped in front of my desk and asked for my response to the next question on the homework sheet.

"I didn't answer it. And I didn't read the chapter," I replied defiantly.

Mr. Allen stopped, looked over his wire-rim frames at me, which I took as an invitation to explain myself.

"I couldn't care less about this rich, White man who wants to live forever," I continued. "Have you been out in our community: the gangs, the poverty, the drugs? I can't understand why anyone would want to live longer so I just didn't read it," I completed with a measure of pride for standing up for myself and for resisting the White middle-class education we were protesting against in the streets.

A pause. A long pause.

Mr. Allen slowly looked back over the homework sheet and moved on to the next student asking the question I had refused to ask. No response to my brief but defiant outburst. Nothing.

Now I began to feel embarrassed for being the only student in the class to create such a scene about the book we were reading. At the end of the class, one of the only other Chicano students in the class walked me out and said, "That was stupid." At that moment, I felt stupid indeed.

***

I was anxious the rest of the day and into the next as I walked back into the class. I took my seat. Mr. Allen, this time, was reading from a new chapter of *The Picture of Dorian Gray* and walking up and down the aisles. He walked by my desk and placed a book on my desk, while continuing to read from Wilde's work without missing a beat.

The book he placed on my desk was *Manchild in the Promised Land* by Claude Brown. The book is centered in Harlem, New York. It is an autobiographical account of Brown as a young man who falls to the vices in the streets: drugs, petty crime, and violence. The book has the real language of the streets, as I was experiencing it, and it was the first time I saw the word "fuck" in a book. At a low point in his life, the young Brown comes upon a young boy who says that he wants to be just like him.

He decides to make a change, to be the role model he wants to be for the young boy. He gets involved in community uplift while exploring his faith and the creed of the Nation of Islam. He never forgets his roots but uses these as an important cultural asset to make a difference in his community.

I devoured the book.

I would stay after class and sometimes come back after school to talk with Mr. Allen about what I had read. When I had finished that book, he asked if I'd ever read *Bless Me, Ultima* by Rudolfo Anaya. I had not. I was immediately hooked. It was as if Ultima, a central character, was taken from observing my very own *abuela*: a *Nueva Mexicana*, an elderly *curandera* who seemed to have a special spiritual power as she walked in the world. Not only did I read it, but also I gave it to my mom and dad to read; within a few short months, nearly all my brothers and sisters read it.

From then on, I actively sought out books that represented the experiences of the Chicano community. Some of the first books of literature I ever owned and bought of my own accord during those days included Oscar Zeta Acosta's *The Revolt of the Cockroach People*, and the compilation of Mexican American literature *La Raza: The Mexican Americans* edited by Stan Steiner.

All along, I felt like I had my own private reading teacher in Mr. Allen, who engaged me with the books I read. He encouraged me to join the class with the next book they would be reading, John Steinbeck's *The Grapes of Wrath*. He assured me that I would find the book engaging. It was indeed that and much more.

***

As the year school year ended, I walked to Mr. Allen's class at the end of the day. As I walked into class, I handed him a paper I had written. It was a report on the book *The Picture of Dorian Gray*. He smiled as I gave him the report. To be true, I still disliked the book and railed against the excesses of the bourgeoisie. But I felt that given the graciousness that Mr. Allen extended to me to help me learn to (love to) read, it was the least I could do to affirm him and his teaching.

Mr. Allen had a gift for me, too. He told me that he knew I might be interested in teaching so he handed me a book: Postman and Weingartner's *Teaching as a Subversive Activity*. At that moment, I understood Mr. Allen even more.

***

Paulo Freire emboldened teachers to promote literacy by recognizing the importance for students to read the world before they learn to read the word. While we often focus on the first part of that sage advice, in schools we often also forget to help students learn to read the word. While the former is a precursor for the latter, both are essential. I've come to recognize that reading the word about the world around you is best of all.

Some forty years later, I think back about that experience and Mr. Allen. I learned that we have to know where our students are coming from, to connect with their identities as a precursor for helping them to consider other kinds of social experiences. I learned that you need to meet students where they are if you are to take them to where you would like them to be. And I learned that some of the best teaching occurs when we engage it as a subversive activity.

FORTY-NINE
Even Kings

By Richard Holinger

George Childs was watching a DVD on his laptop when Jill Simon whirled into the English office after class.

"I had a student walk out on me today."

George ignored her. Renee Jacobs, grading papers, merely grunted. George hoped his ear buds would protect him from conversation.

"First time that's happened to me. Not a word. Just ups and leaves." Jill let her books and papers drop onto her desk like a student wanting attention. "Now I have to call the dean to see if the kid checked into his office. Probably hid out in the john instead."

"Be grateful." George pulled out his ear buds. He had to teach class anyway, so why not give his chairperson what she wanted, some feedback. "One less pissant to deal with. Why don't any of my guys ever just say 'Screw it' and take off?"

Terrence Smith, George's slightly elder colleague who annually threatened to retire, strolled in and took the prestigious desk under the room's one small window. The old brick building, once a girls' reformatory, though stately, needed more light. Outside, the quad's one oak tree stood half-denuded of yellow leaves.

"Anyone else," Jill pressed, "have Ricardo Alvarez in class or study hall?"

"Alvarez?" Terrence swiveled in his CEO office desk chair he bragged came from a garage sale. "What about Alvarez?"

"He walked out!" Jill's voice rose at the scrap of recognition. "His group was over by the heater, but the blower muffled their voices, so who knows what they were saying. Suddenly Alvarez stands up, grabs his books, and heads for the door. As he goes by my desk, I try to lighten

193

things up, so I say, 'What, you don't like Twain?' He doesn't answer. He doesn't stop."

"That's the kid," Terrence said. "In study hall yesterday, a bunch of kids in the corner were jazzed up about something. I went over to tell them to shut up, and one of them says, 'It's all on Alvarez!' and snickers. I told him to knock it off and open a book. Alvarez was a few desks away pretending to read *Huck*."

George pulled up his tie, threw on his corduroy coat, and cradled the books he needed for class. The bell rang as he walked into his classroom. The juniors were in their desks, their hum no louder than a refrigerator's. As he turned to the seating chart and scanned the room for absences, he caught a voice say, "Alvarez." Looking in that direction, he saw Rodriguez leaning over listening to Del Toro, the only Hispanics in his five sections.

"'Sup, guys?" George asked, glancing around the room to give the impression that taking attendance held his interest far more than their covert conversation.

"Nuthin.'" Rodriguez straightened in his chair.

"Yeah, nuthin,'" Del Toro said, then smiled. "An' we not tell it to you."

"A secret saved is a secret earned." George sent the absence form in and picked up Garrison Keillor's anthology of poems he read from to start class. Poetry, if any good, relaxed and readied the boys, focused their attention better than "Be quiet," or "Pay attention." The poem bookmarked for today belonged to Gary Snyder.

"Anyone ever heard of Jack Kerouac?" he prompted. No hands. He clapped a hand to his forehead, an exaggerated show of exasperation. "*On the Road*?" Blank stares. "Not that I'm asking you to read it; I want to keep my job." Now that he had their attention, most eyes meeting his, he could get to the point. "Gary Snyder belonged to the Beat Generation of the Fifties. Nineteen-fifties. They preceded hippies." Smiles. They'd heard of hippies. Probably a parent or grandparent had confessed to being one. "Snyder studied Zen Buddhism in Japan. Anyone know what Zen is? Buddhism?"

Stan Rowley raised his hand. "The Buddha was this fat, cross-legged guy in a robe. There's a humongous statue of him at the Ay-shun Amer-i-can restaurant we go to."

Murmurs. Suppressed chuckles. Glances around the room. Damn, George thought, here we go again. I have to go there.

"Making fun of people who look or sound different than us, Mr. Rowley, whether it's Asians, Goths, or gays, implies a prejudice. Prejudice isn't hate; it's ignorance. Not understanding someone can lead to fearing them, so we concoct little boxes to contain them all. To control them. Or try to."

"Whud I say?" Rowley spreads his arms in mock innocence. "I said 'Asian Americans.'"

George wanted to remain calm, but when know-it-all prigs echoed their parents' racist crap, it pissed him off. His students wore short haircuts and blue-blazer and khaki-pants uniform obediently, and for that George gave thanks; sartorial conformity did help discipline. Too bad, though, they didn't show a little more gumption when it came to questioning antiquated attitudes regarding equality. He'd hammer home Thoreau when they got to him next week, pound *Civil Disobedience* into their little robotic minds.

"Racism and bigotry are not natural. It's learned. Remember Douglass? Mrs. Auld and the white boys he played with instinctively liked him and wanted to help him. You're taught by example and lecture to denigrate others, just like Mrs. Auld getting schooled by her slave-owning husband. She learns from him to disparage Douglass, and after he instructs her in good slave-training techniques and attitudes, she bullies him. She gives into her husband's teaching. She had to unlearn the consideration that she naturally wanted to show Douglass."

George paused and looked around the room. He had their attention, and he didn't want to waste it. "Anyone who attacks someone with racial, ethnic, or religious slurs I'd call ignorant and cowardly."

Rowley smirked. "You say bullies are all the same. That means you're just like them, right? Saying they're all alike?"

"No, not at all," George blurted as the class responded with titters to the red meat Rowley the Instigator threw into their cage. "I'm just saying . . ."

"Do they kick out Spencer?" Del Toro leaned forward.

"He's the one who hassled Alvarez?"

"One of them. The biggest one."

Students knew more than the faculty when it came to crimes and punishments, and George usually knew less than most of the faculty. This could be his chance to dance with the bride first — and nail a kid for bullying.

"What'd Spencer do?"

"Call him things. Call him things in class and in the hall. Kick his car in the parking lot."

"Yeah," added Rodriguez.

"Can I see you two guys for a second after class?"

"You doan know everything," Rodriguez said. "There is things you doan know."

"Hey, Mr. C," Rowley called from the back row. "Will you be judging Spencer based on prejudice, then? I mean, if you don't know what he did? That's bigotry. You said it yourself."

If George broke off discussion now, he'd be retreating from Rowley's Pickett's Charge. The kid wasn't defending Spencer; he was defending the pleasure a racist rant afforded, the good feeling of heaping his grief, frustration, and failings on an outsider.

"No courtroom has ever heard the whole truth, Mr. Rowley. Not even O.J.'s, ancient history to you. Sentences are routinely handed down on evidence presented, including circumstantial evidence. That means what probably happened, based on available credible information. But I take your point. We can't judge anyone until enough facts are gathered to get a somewhat coherent picture of what happened."

"Gonna kick him out, I bet." Rowley slumped in his desk to empha-size his dissatisfaction with the school's lynch-mob mentality. "Gonna use him as an example."

"Back to the poem," George said, and lost himself to Snyder's conver-sational, rhythmic lines about bucking hay in a far western state, about a man who began working ranches at seventeen, and at seventy realized he'd wasted his whole life doing something he swore he wouldn't do. The poem reflected George's three decades of teaching, during his first stormy years promising himself he'd find something else, but after the waters smoothed, he had coasted through middle age until retirement loomed like Tennyson's horizon into which he sailed Ulysses.

After class, George corralled Rodriguez and Del Toro by the window. "Look. You wanna help Alvarez? Tell the dean what you know about how Spencer bullied Alvarez. Today."

"Maybe," said Del Toro.

"Okay," said Rodriguez.

"You're good to do this," he told them. "Now get to your next class."

The rest of the day dragged. The mess with Rowley weighed him down. George could have dealt with it better, talked with less fervor, used better examples. After the last bell, he waited half an hour, then called Dean Mackey.

"Hey, Harve, did Rodriguez and Del Toro stop by to talk to you about this Spencer? He's apparently been harassing Alvarez."

After a brief silence, Mackey said, "You didn't hear?"

"Hear what?"

"Those two are up for a disciplinary board meeting. They started a fight at lunch. They said kids were winging food at them from Spencer's table, but they threw the first punches, so they're culpable."

"I got them to speak to you about Spencer bugging Alvarez. Word gets around fast."

"We'll deal with the bullying after we meet about their fighting. Whatever the punishment they get—detentions, community service, sus-pension, expulsion—if they rat out Spencer, it'll just be read as retalia-tion."

"What about Alvarez? Sounds like Spencer's been pulling this stuff long before the fight began. Deal with things chronologically, and you have to confront the bullying first."

"A fight at lunch beats out harassment. Stick and stones, right? We'll get to your issue, but more of the student body knows about the fists thrown than the hassling."

"It's not my issue, Harve. The issue is protecting Alvarez." George stopped. Why bother? "I want to speak at the disciplinary hearing on behalf of those guys. I know you like to hold court as soon after the infraction as possible, so let me know, even if I've got class. Write that down."

"We got a lot on our plate, George. Looks pretty black and white to me. The whole dining room saw the fight, and there's tons of kids we have to interview who were at Spencer's table who witnessed who started it. It's not like you're going to tell us it didn't happen."

"Yeah, well, anyway. If you can fit me in, I'd appreciate it."

Next day, taking roll in fourth period, George saw the Hispanics were no-shows. "Anyone know where Rodriguez and Del Toro are?"

"Disciplinary hearing," Rowley called, slouching farther down than usual. "Started a fight at lunch yesterday. D'ja hear about that, Mr. C? Both of 'em started wailin' on Spencer for no good reason."

"I heard there was an altercation."

"Yeah," Rowley growled, "your altercation made it necessary for Spencer's buds, including me, to pull the two animals offa him. They'da killed him if I hadn't been there."

"You're a prince, Mr. Rowley." George's stomach tightened. "I'm glad you saw fit to reinstate justice where injustice prevailed. Someday," George hesitated, debating whether to continue. "Someday," he said again, then plunged in, "Someday you might save the whales, be the first Caucasian leader of the NAACP. Or an advocate for renewable energy, and a major financial contributor to NPR."

"What's NPR?"

"Not Particularly Relevant," Crawford, Spencer's sidekick, snickered. "That's what my dad calls it."

"Your dad's a genius," George said. He'd gone too far, but it felt too good to stop. "You and Rowley should be a team. Fight for gay marriage and a woman's right to choose. The Lovable Liberals you can call yourselves. Go on Letterman and bond with Dave. Change the nation into a socialist dictatorship, the impoverished and needy college students running the country through their inordinate demands on the evil upper two-percenters, to which elite club surely your parents belong. Boycott BP and Wal-Mart."

He walked up and down the aisles to work off the adrenaline overload that threatened to make his voice quaver and his jaw shake. "I look forward to reading in our school's alumni magazine your future accomplishments. Married with children, all white as snowy linen, earning over a couple mil a month in jobs handed to you by hard-working fathers, your wives volunteering at local homeless shelters supported with generous donations to help you feel connected to the underclass without soiling your mitts by shaking their hands."

At the window, through the gray day, George saw the boardroom window lit. He imagined Rodriguez and Del Toro getting drilled by faculty members, deans, and a headmaster who wouldn't, because they couldn't, fully comprehend what prompted the fight. Who sitting there would believe a couple of Hispanics? Hell, leaning back in those high-backed faux-leather chairs, maybe he himself, not knowing what he knows, would not give credence to their story.

That's why he needed to be there corroborating their side of things, the truth as he knew it. After thirty-plus years in the classroom, he had a pretty good sense of when kids were lying and when they were talking from the heart. Rodriguez and Del Toro were good kids. They wanted to help Alvarez, and now they were going to pay for their goodness.

He turned from the window and looked at his class. Having gotten their teacher to freak out on them, the boys looked ready to explode with mirth. The whispers stopped as his eyes took in each student. If he left immediately, if he could arrange with the dean's secretary to find someone to take this and his following class, maybe he could make it to the board meeting before they voted on disciplinary action. He could explain what he'd heard in class yesterday, plead to the board to take into account Spencer's manipulative grape, malt ball, or French fry thrown to antagonize Rodriguez and Del Toro. George could, at the very least, get the board to mitigate whatever punishment they decided to mete out. He could make a difference to these two boys, show them there is justice and fairness in the world.

The class had calmed down. Even Rowley was sitting up, surely hoping his teacher's rant would continue. George, however, had regained his composure and looked ready to hand out demerits or deliver a lecture on decorum. He went to his desk and picked up the poetry anthology. Running his fingers down the titles on the table of contents page, he found the one he wanted.

"You've already heard this one," he said. "But it might be appropriate, given what we've been discussing."

It wasn't a heavy, profound poem, but light verse called "Routine," by Guiterman, because George needed to change the mood. His tirade had done nothing to change Rowley and Crawford into enlightened transcendentalists. If anything, it encouraged their hostility, cemented their archaic values.

"'No matter what we are and who, / Some duties everyone must do: // A poet puts aside his wreath / To wash his hands and brush his teeth . . .'" He had their attention. They weren't expecting a ditty. "'And even Earls / Must comb their curls, // And even kings / have underthings.'" The poem ended, George waited a beat, giving it a chance to work.

"Underneath our talk, swagger, and robes, we're all human beings. No matter how much money we make, how elegantly our clothes hang, how white or black or yellow or chartreuse or wrinkled our skin is. If you remember nothing else from this course this year, remember this: '. . . And even kings have underthings.'"

George looked at the classroom's closed door, looked at his students staring at the crazy poet-philosopher, and decided the hell with it.

"Get out your books," he said, and began to write on the whiteboard as he delivered the instructions. "Open to page 660. Write out the answers to questions two, three, four, and five. Review the Dunbar poems if you need to. Anyone talks or gets out of line can look forward to my wrath."

Leaving the classroom, he left the door open. In the English office, he found Terrence, feet on the heater, ear buds plugged in, his senior anthology open in his lap.

"Hey, Terrence. Can you do me a favor?"

His friend looked up. "No."

"Thanks. Take my class for a few minutes. The only kids who might give you trouble are two kids in back, Rowley and Crawford."

Terrence shut the book. "Bastard."

"I might be. Who really knows for sure? Thanks again."

On his way to the hearing, George wondered how long it would take for Rowley's and Crawford's parents to call the headmaster complaining their sons had been verbally abused by their English teacher. What the hell, George thought. It was worth it. It was so worth it, he smiled, and his laugh erupted as he passed the headmaster's secretary who looked at him strangely just before he knocked on the closed boardroom door.

Section Questions: Subversive Teaching and Learning

1. In "How I Learned to Read the Word" by Francesco Rios, a teacher picks a book that will reach a student and thus connects the printed word to that student. With more and more standardized curriculum, how can teachers reach students today? What do you see in schools, classrooms that show how teachers resist a uniform, scripted way of teaching to connect with their students?
2. In the end of "Even Kings," George, the teacher, decides to stand up for a student. It may mean his job. Think of situations in school where you or someone you know has been willing to risk something.
3. What are ways that both students and teachers and principals resist, connect, celebrate, and challenge the systems that oppress them? How can we create a school system based on celebrating strengths, differences, and resilience?